Literary TEXAS

A Guide to the State's Bookish Destinations

from the editors of
Lone Star Literary Life

BLUE ROAD BOOKS • LUBBOCK, TEXAS
AN IMPRINT OF BOOKADELPHIA
BOOKADELPHIA.COM
2016

Literary Texas:
A Guide to the State's Bookish Destinations
Copyright © 2016 Lone Star Literary Life

All rights reserved. No portion of this book may be reproduced in any form or by any means, including electronic storage and retrieval systems, except for brief passages excerpted for review or critical purposes, without the explicit prior written permission of the publisher.

Published by Boldface Books, an imprint of Bookadelphia

www.Bookadelphia.com

This book was set in the Abril and Acumin typefaces for Adobe InDesign CC on the Macintosh computer.

ISBN 978-1-935619-07-9 (trade paperback)

978-1-935619-08-6 (ebook)

www.LoneStarLiterary.com

Contents

Foreword From the Editors 5

1 Austin 7

2 Houston 20

3 Dallas 28

4 Abilene 35

5 Permian Basin/Midland-Odessa   45

6 San Antonio   53

7 Fort Worth   61

8 El Paso 69

9 Denton 77

10 Waco   83

11 Honorable Mention

   Lubbock 90

   Rio Grande Valley 93

   Big Bend 96

12 Readers' Favorite Bookstores   98

13 Major Book Events in Texas 118

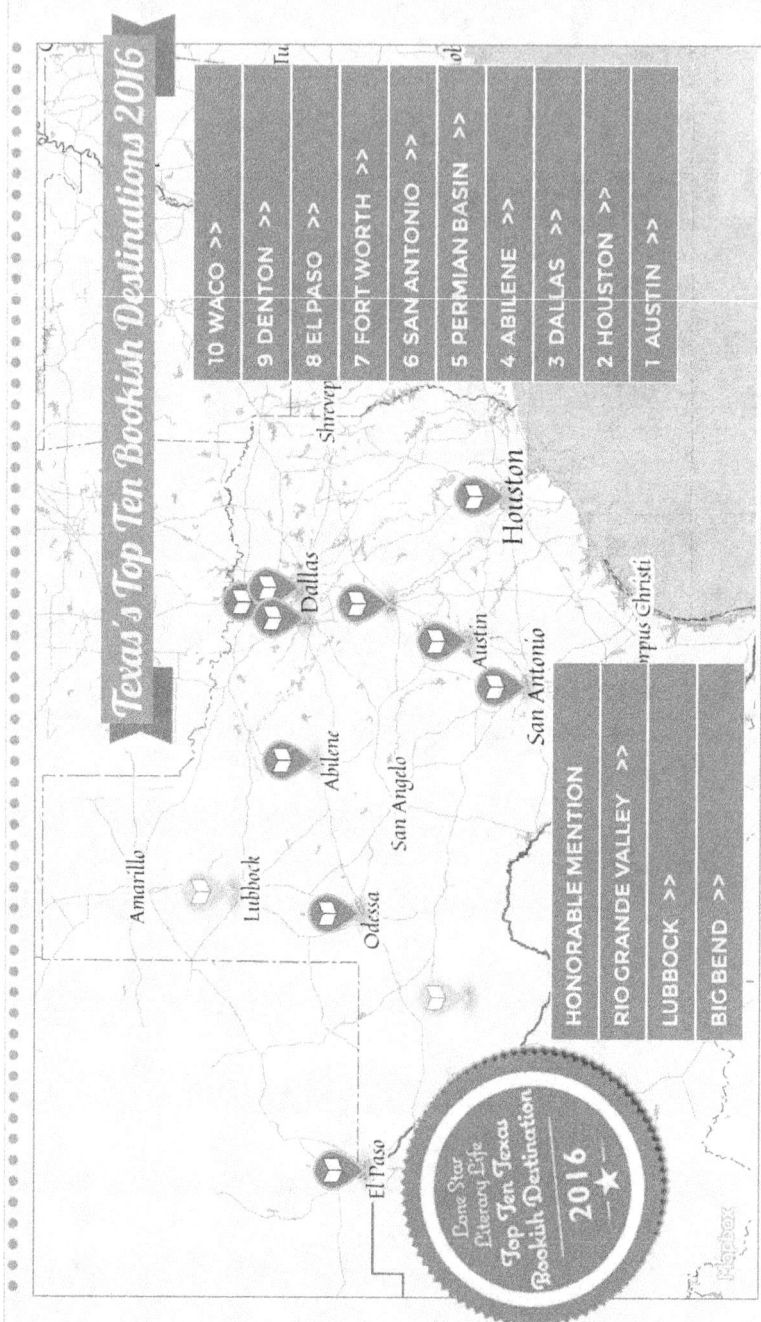

FROM THE EDITORS

What makes a place a Top Texas Bookish Destination?

MOST OF THE READERS AND WRITERS we know, far from being the sort to only haunt the recesses of their town's library or curl up on the couch when the sun's shining, like to get out and visit the places they've read about. Or the places that inspire them.

For the second year in a row Lone Star Literary Life polled our staff—in a most informal but serious way—about the places in Texas that fueled their bookish imaginations. What literary destinations called to them to get out the map, get in the car, and go? Was it a whim to attend a festival, a desire to follow in a favorite author's footsteps, an urge to browse the shelves of an unusual bookshop, a hunt for a novel's real-life inspiration?

It didn't take long for our list to grow. In fact, things got a bit heated as we tried to decide which destination might trump another — especially as we applied our own growing knowledge of attractions new and old to updating our 2015 list. You'll see a few new entries this year, as new events, updated libraries, and big new books play a huge part in our determinations. We noted alluring locales from the piney woods to the prairies, in big cities and small, from the coast to the mountains. We ranked and researched and ranked some more.

Our writeups and rankings are highly subjective, we grant you. The book scene is ever-changing, and we have to own up to not always being able to mention every recent development, or to acknowledge every worthy author, publisher, or bookstore in our pages.

Though we concentrated primarily on those aspects of literary life that make a place "visitable," we are striving to capture the bookish flavor and fabric of each place that also depend on the ongoing products of its writers behind closed doors, or the experiences shared by locals that visitors can only occasionally tap into. We promise to work harder to discover and share more next year!

All we can hope is that Lone Star Lit readers will find something here they didn't know before—and even if they have to just toss all ten names in a hat and take turns choosing the next goal for a road trip, they'll enjoy what they find when they get there.

Read on, share this issue with a friend, and send us your own thoughts: info@LoneStarLiterary.com.

TOP BOOKISH DESTINATION #1

> O. Henry knew it in the 1800s; the Texas Book Festival knew it when it celebrated 20 years in Austin: the state's capital is the undisputed center of Texas literary life.

Austin

A NUMBER OF NEWCOMERS arrived on the literary scene in Austin in 2015, as the state's number one bookish destination continues to grow in its venues for connoisseurs of letters, words, and books.

Texas Center for the Book

In fall 2015 the Texas Center for the Book (TCB) moved to Austin from Dallas, where the Dallas Public Library had hosted the organization since its inception in 1987. The TCB, located at the **Lorenzo de Zavala State Archives and Library Building** in Austin, was established to stimulate public interest in books, reading and libraries and encourages the study of the written word to the more than 26 million residents in the State of Texas.

One of fifty state centers affiliated with the Center for the Book in the Library of Congress, the TCB is a nonprofit organization under the direction of the Texas State Library and Archives Commission and is guided by library professionals, educators, authors, publishers and booksellers who provide support to their shared mission of promoting a love of literature throughout the Lone Star State. The TCB sponsors special exhibits, literary programs, creative writing contests, lectures and symposia, and publications. It promotes the educational and cultural role of the book; the history of books and printing; authorship and writing; libraries; publishing and preservations of books; reading and literacy.

The TCB and the Texas State Archives and Library are among the many government and university sites in the state's capitol that welcome visitors regularly. Bookish travelers to Austin will find literary wonders in store at the LBJ Presidential Library, the LLILAS (Lozano Long Institute of Latin American Studies) Benson Collection (below) and the Dolph Briscoe Center for American History, and UT's Perry-Castañeda Library, all on the UT campus, as well as the Austin History Center, a unit of the public library.

Austin Public Library's many locales and programs

In Austin, one of the bookish newcomers might even come to you. In November the Austin Public Library debuted its first human-powered mobile library, unbound: sin fronteras, which shares books, information and online resources with the community at non-traditional venues. The unbound: sin fronteras trike and trailer pops up around Austin at community events, washaterias, or even city parks. Funded by the Austin Public Library and the Austin Transportation Department's Active Transportation Program (formerly the City of Austin Bicycle Program), the unbound: sin fronteras fleet is made up of a cargo trike from Haley Trikes in Philadelphia and a custom-built trailer by local builder Saila Bicycles. Both are hand-painted by Red Rider Studios, which recently relocated to Taylor, Texas. The trike and trailer were assembled in Austin at East Side Pedal Pushers.

The Austin Public Library system includes its Faulk Central Library at 800 Guadalupe Street, and twenty public library branches that host everything from genealogy classes to the Austin Poetry Society's monthly gatherings to the Recycled Reads secondhand bookstore. But stay tuned for library news later this year: The **New Central Library,** facing Lady Bird Lake, will open in November 2016 as the first "library for the future" in the United States and only the second in the world.

Learn book arts

The Austin Book Arts Center (above), housed in the im-*press*-ive Flatbed building at 2832 E. Martin Luther King, opened at its new location in fall 2015 with a mission to engage people of all ages in creative, interpretive, and educational experiences related to the arts of the book. Beginning last fall, and drawing on the expertise of longtime book-arts specialists in the area as well as Austin émigré from Houston's Printing Museum **Amanda Stevenson,** ABAC has offered workshops in letterpress printing, bookbinding, papermaking, typography, book history and design, and various arts of the book. In addition, ABAC provided access to equipment for qualified users during regularly scheduled Open Studios. Through its activities, ABAC seeks to advance the book as a vital contemporary art form, preserve the traditional and robust crafts related to making books, promote the contemporary arts of making books, inspire diverse artists and learners, and engage the community in creative, interpretive, and educational experiences, including the improvement of literacy for people of all ages.

And if you're a fan of vintage letter craft—or a poet—check out the Typewriter Rodeo, a hardy group of writers-for-hire who create ad hoc compositions on old Royals and Underwoods.

Texas Book Festival

One Austin tradition that has bridged old and new is the Texas Book Festival, which begins its third decade this fall (the exact weekend is always coordinated with the UT away football schedule); 2016 dates are Nov. 5-6). A free annual book fair held on the grounds and premises of the state capitol and other nearby venues, the festival was established in 1995 by **Laura Bush** (then first lady of Texas) and **Mary Margaret Farabee,** wife of former state senator Ray Farabee.

Featuring hundreds of authors, performers, and publishers each year, the festival benefits the state's public library system, promotes the joy of reading, and honors Texas authors. With the assistance of honorary chairman and librarian Mrs. Bush, and a dedicated task force, the festival has grown to be one of the largest in the nation, and it's hosted more than 3,000 authors since its introduction.

The Texas Book Festival also hosts other events throughout the year. For an annual calendar of recurring events in Austin, and the current year's dates as soon as they're posted, refer to Lone Star Literary Life's Go page. In Austin, check out the Texas Teen Book Festival, **the** Jewish Book Fair, **the** New Fiction Confab, **the** African American Book Festival; Austin International Poetry Festival, and Poetry at Round Top, to name a few.

Indie bookstores, chain bookstores

Austin is blessed with a bounty of bookstores, including indies **BookPeople, BookWoman, Malvern Books, Farewell Books, Resistencia Bookstore, South Congress Books, Austin Books & Comics, MonkeyWrench Books, and Brave New Books.** Read more in-depth descriptions of these bastions of books at the Texas Book Festival website and five Barnes & Nobles, six Half Price Books stores, and a Mardel Christian Bookstore. All feature regularly events for the literary enthusiast.

BookPeople alone hosts more than 300 (yes, three hundred) events annually, with authors far and near.

For popular touring authors—such as recent readers **Stephen King** and former president **Jimmy Carter**—space may be limited, and the store issues advance free tickets for these. But even if you can't make it in person to a signing, BookPeople provides an online pre-ordering service for signed copies.

BookWoman, on North Lamar, recently celebrated forty years in business—making it one of only a handful of feminist bookstores still thriving in North America. Owner **Susan Post** was named Austin's "Best Feminist Flamekeeper" by the *Austin Chronicle* in 2014; the store has made the *Chronicle's* "best" lists in numerous categories over the years.

In the spoken-word realm, there's a lot to hear in Austin, including the Neo-Soul Poetry Slam (every Thursday at **Mr. Catfish & More**), the Austin Poetry Slam (Tuesdays at the **Spider House Café and Ballroom**), and the Spoken and Heard (Open Mic poetry) series (**Kick Butt Coffee,** Sunday nights).

Every first Tuesday of the month, Austinites gather around to hear writers and authors read one page of a project they're working on at the One Page Salon at the **Whip In** (1950 S IH-35), a performance space-cum-Indian food restaurant–cum wine-and-Asian food purveyor-cum-biergarten. The projects vary in style and type. Prose, poetry, plays, novels, short stories, screen plays, anything involving the written word is welcome. The concept of One Page Salon started several years ago when writer **Owen Egerton** and his wife wanted to hang out with fellow creative types, drink wine, and share ideas. Fortunately, they had to look no further for a host than his favorite writing spot, Whip In. Owner **Dipak Topiwala** has been a longtime supporter of Egerton and his work.

Literary visitors and Austin's university campuses

Austin's a world-class university city, of course, and that means frequent opportunities to catch a reading by visiting writers at **UT-Austin, St. Edward's University, Austin Community College,** and other institutions. UT's Harry Ransom Center for the Humanities, which last year added the papers of the late Nobel Prize winning author **Gabriel García Márquez** to its lengthy roster of literary archives, maintains a renowned collection of rare books (including a Gutenberg Bible and three Shakespeare First Folios) and holds more than 42 million manuscripts. The Center mounts public exhibitions year-round from its collections (a recent show celebrated 150 years of ***Alice's Adventures in Wonderland***). While the HRC is primarily a research institution and use of its collections must be arranged in advance, public tours are offered at regular times, several days a week; no reservation is required.

The **Michener Center for Writers,** a top-ranked MFA program, accepts fellows to study and write with dozens of resident and visiting faculty in fiction, poetry, playwriting or screenwriting. (Michener Chair in Fiction **Elizabeth McCracken** last year won the $20,000 Story Prize from the Chisholm Foundation for her latest collection of stories, ***Thunderstruck***.)

Austin's authors

Other well-known living authors from Austin or with Austin connections—and this is only a brief sampling of local talent indeed—include **Jeff Abbott, Sarah Bird, Gary Cartwright, Oscar Casares, Elizabeth Crook, Kinky Friedman, Stephen Harrigan, Bethany Hegedus, David Heymann, Rolando Hinojosa-Smith, Skip Hollandsworth, Cynthia**

Leitech Smith, Nikki Loftin, James Magnuson (director of the Michener Center), Jan Reid, Mary Helen Specht, John Spong, Liz Garon Scanlon, Kip Stratton, Jesse Sublett, Andres Tijerina, Toni Tipton-Martin, and Lawrence Wright. The Austin Public Library maintains a useful, comprehensive list: www.austinlinks.com/austin_media/austin_writers.html

Past literary lights of Austin include western writer **J. Frank Dobie** and the newsman-storyteller **O. Henry,** the onetime Austin resident William Sidney Porter, who crowned the state capital "City of the Violet Crown."

You can visit O. Henry's relocated Victorian-style house at 409 East 5th Street; the house serves as a museum dedicated to the author's life and career during his Austin years, and the organization hosts monthly readings and an annual pun contest.

WRITERS'
LEAGUE
OF TEXAS

The Writers' League of Texas and other writers' resources

For learning experiences accessible to the wider writing public, join the Writers' League of Texas and sign up for their workshops, newsletters, conference, and contests. Founded in 1981 as the Austin Writers' League, the organization expanded its scope in 2000 to serve a statewide population of writers and authors.

In recent years Austin has played home to a burgeoning enclave of young adult, middle grade, and children's authors. Four local chapters of the **Society of Children's Book Writers and Illustrators** (SCBWI) are known for fostering a close-knit community of children's book creators. It meets monthly and holds workshops and critique and networking opportunities throughout the year. The organization also runs an annual conference for all levels of creators.

Austin's also home to the Texas Institute of Letters; three chapters of the **Romance Writers of America,** two chapters of **Sisters in Crime**, a chapter of **Mystery Writers of America,** and more than a dozen critique groups in the region that are open to newcomers. (Check them out on Lone Star Literary Life's Write page.)

If you like to learn about the writing craft when you travel, you'll want to check out the Writing Barn (above, at a "Words and Wine Wednesday" reading with novelist Mary Helen Specht). Situated on seven-and-a-half wooded acres in south Austin, this rural-chic facility under the oaks provides a peaceful retreat for writers a short drive from downtown and hosts a slate of workshops, talks, seminars, and meetings.

And when you're ready to plug into the publishing scene, you'll find myriad opportunities in Austin. From the **University of Texas Press,** which publishes regional trade books and art books in addition to its core of scholarly titles, to a flourishing trend of independent and small presses and journals, there's plenty to learn and enjoy.

Plan your visit

In addition to the statewide coverage of book events and authors news in **Lone Star Literary Life** each week, and the reviews in the Sunday *Austin American-Statesman,* when you're traveling to Austin be sure to check out the *American-Statesman's* ***Austin 360*** and the ***Austin Chronicle*** to plan your bookish itinerary.

For more information on lodging, eats & drinks, and other visitor information, go to AustinTexas.org. To learn more about the area's history, visit the Texas Hill Country Trail Region website.

TOP BOOKISH DESTINATION #2

The city named for the first president of the Texas Republic has lots more to offer than big oil and big money. Check out its bookstores, museums, and events!

Houston

HOUSTON LAYS CLAIM to the earliest literary contribution about Texas. After running aground near Galveston Island in 1528, Spanish explorer **Álvar Núñez Cabeza de Vaca** and his companions wandered more than 2,400 miles of the region that would centuries later become Texas. He published the account of his travels in 1542 as the *Relación*, the first literary work with Texas as its subject.

Houston's bookstores and more

These days, more than two dozen bookstores don the Houston literary landscape. We count more than twenty-five new, used, independent, chain, and specialty stores in Houston proper, not to mention destination-worthy stores in nearby locales such as Conroe, Galveston, Spring, and the Woodlands. Houston's Brazos Bookstore, (below, submitted photo), Blue Willow Books, Murder by the Book, River Oaks Bookstore, Katy Budget Books, and Kaboom! Bookstore, in addition to a dozen **Barnes & Noble, Mardel,** and **Half Price Books** outlets, are among those regularly featuring touring and local authors for readings and signings.

But bookstores are only the tip of the iceberg, so to speak, when it comes to Houston's cool literary scene.

Inprint Houston, a non-profit organization dedicated to inspiring readers and writers, fulfills its mission through the nationally renowned Margarett Root Brown Reading Series, the Cool Brains! Reading Series for Young People, literary and educational activities in the community that demonstrate the value and impact of creative writing, and support for the University of Houston Creative Writing Program.

Writespace is Houston's newest writing center. Founded in April 2014 as a grass-roots literary arts organization created by writers, for writers, Writespace supports writers of all genres, including literary fiction, poetry, science fiction, fantasy, mystery, and young adult. Through their weekly writing workshops led by some of Houston's finest writing teachers, Writespace seeks to give writers who can't afford to earn an MFA in creative writing the same high-quality training and mentorship opportunities available through MFA programs.

Writespace held its first literary festival, Writefest, Feb. 22-28, 2016, in Silver Street Studios. The festival included four-day writers' workshops, panels, presentations, and a literary journal fair featuring *McSweeney's*, *Nano Fiction*, *Gulf Coast*, and more. As well as hosting its first literary festival and regular weekly workshops, Writespace offers manuscript consultations, write-ins, readings and open mics, and classes and private lessons for young writers.

Lone Star College will host the Lone Star Book Festival, a two-day event featuring nationally and internationally known fiction and non-fiction authors, April 8 and 9, 2016. The festival will be held at the LSC-Kingwood campus, about twelve miles from Houston's city limits. Former Houston Astros manager **Larry Dierker** will be the luncheon keynote speaker and former Houston Oilers QB **Dan Pastorini,** author of *Taking Flak: My Life in the Fast Lane* is featured on a panel. More than 125 authors in almost every genre will appear at one of the largest book festivals for the Houston area ever.

Bragging Rights?

The city sibling rivalry between Dallas and Houston has been around, well, for about as long as when Cabeza de Vaca washed up on the Gulf Coast shore and headed inland. In fact, one book titled *Bragging Rights* by Houston author **John DeMers** and Dallas author **Carolyn Kneese,** published by Houston's Bright Sky Press, showcases their civic one-upmanship. DeMers is also known to make mischief as a mystery novelist, cookbook author, and radio host. Other influential book publishers, including **Arte Público Press, John M. Hardy Publishing**, and **Mutabilis Press,** are based in Houston.

Speaking of the gulf coast. . . begun by **Donald Barthelme** and **Phillip Lopate,** *Gulf Coast* is the nationally distributed journal housed within the University of Houston's English Department, home to one of the U.S.'s top ranked creative writing programs. The journal spent its nascent years (1982–85) as *Domestic Crude,* a name that nodded to the major industry of the Houston area. It was a 64-page (magazine-formatted) student-run publication, with editorial advising coming from Lopate, who also contributed work to the first issues.

In 1986, the name Gulf Coast premiered. It stuck. After some experimenting, the journal found its dimensions and, eventually, its audience. The journal has since moved beyond the student body of the University of Houston and into the larger world. The readership of the print journal currently exceeds 3,000, with more and more coming to its ever-expanding website. The print journal comes out each April and October.

A museum for book lovers

Located in Houston's vibrant North Montrose District, The Printing Museum was founded in 1979 by **Raoul Beasley, Vernon P. Hearn, Don Piercy,** and **J. V. Burnham,** four printers with passions for preserving their vast collections and sharing them with the community. The museum was chartered in 1981 and had its official opening in 1982 with **Dr. Hans Halaby,** director of the Gutenberg Museum in Mainz, Germany, cutting the ribbon. In 2012, the museum rebranded as the Printing Museum.

Houston books, Houston authors

The lion of the Lone Star Literary scene, venerable **Larry McMurtry,** has written more than one ode to the influence of Rice University and Houston upon his work, and the Space City has also skyrocketed a multitude of authors onto the national stage. Houston writers include **Laura Furman, Thomas Thompson, Attica Locke, Chris Candor, Kimberly Meyer, Antonya Nelson, poet Sarah Cortez, Donald Barthelme, Sr., Thomas McNeely, Mat Johnson, Katherine Center,** and **Ashley Hope Perez,** among others.

In 1981 McMurtry famously wrote the controversial essay, "Ever a Bridegroom: Reflections on the Failure of Texas Writing," faulting Texas authors for having ignored the life of the cities. McMurtry has set three novels in his beloved Houston, Texas's largest city.

The Blind Bull (1952) by Rice creative writing professor and program founder **George Williams** won first prize from the Texas Institute of Letters and seemed to kick off the legacy of letters in Houston. Some of the more notable students Williams helped influence include **David Westheimer, William Goyen, Larry McMurtry, John Graves, James P. Miller,** and **James Korges.**

Public Poetry is a nonprofit organization whose mission is to expose people to good poetry and to promote this art form by taking poetry public. Public Poetry collaborates with community partners such as the City of Houston/Houston Public Library, the Museum of Fine Arts Houston, the Menil Collection, and Writers in the Schools/WITS to promote poetry in public venues and to present award winning poets to diverse audiences. Other collaborative partners include UH-Downtown, News 88.7 KUHF & Classical 91.7 KUHA, Mutabilis Press, and Houston Media Source. Public Poetry originates groundbreaking programs that introduce a roster of award winning poets to audiences citywide, free of charge. Since launching in April 2011, Public Poetry has been in 17 different venues, from inside the loop to beyond the beltway, organized 53 free poetry events, with over 130 poets participating, including a US poet laureate, four Texas state poets laureate and two Pulitzer Prize nominees together with local, regional, and several national poets.

Gulf Coast Reads: On the Same Page is an annual regional reading initiative focused on promoting the simultaneous reading or listening to a selected title by those living along the upper Texas Gulf Coast. Each year a representative committee of librarians from the area selects a book that has a broad appeal to adults in their communities, is recognized in authoritative and professional journals, is available in multiple formats from print to downloadable content, and preferably, is available in multiple languages. The title should also lend itself to related programming about the themes or subjects within.

The reading initiative's goal is to encourage communities to read the same title during the month of October in order to encourage readers to come together in discussions about it with neighbors, co-workers, friends, and their families, as well as in classrooms and in libraries throughout the region. Last year's Gulf Coast Reads selection was *The Promise* by **Ann Weisgarber.**

Plan your visit

For more information on lodging, eats & drinks, and other visitor information, go to VisitHoustonTexas.com. To learn more about the area's history, visit the Texas Independence Trail Region website.

Above: Blue Willow Bookshop (submitted photo)

TOP BOOKISH DESTINATION #3

From the notorious Texas School Book Depository —now a world-class museum — to the Wild Detectives and the Deep Vellum Bookstore, there's lots of literary life in the Big D.

Dallas

IF YOU TALK TO DALLAS READERS, authors, booksellers, and librarians, they'll tell it's a very different literary locale than it was two years ago.

Insiders largely attribute the growing literary scene to the independent bookstores and venues that have sprouted around the Dallas area of late. The Wild Detectives (right, submitted photo), established in early 2014 by Javier Garcia del Moral and Paco Vique, is a coffee-booze-book stop in Bishop Arts District.

Publisher Will Evans's Deep Vellum, a publishing house known for its international translations, opened its own bookstore, Deep Vellum Books, in 2015. There's also Serj Books, which vends coffee, local food, and a small but eclectic selection of hand-picked titles.

Not just indies

The country's third largest bookstore chain, Half Price Books, is headquartered in Dallas, and its Mothership/flagship store is also a must-stop for any author touring a book in the Big D vicinity. It's worth mentioning that Half Price Books has 19 stores across Dallas's myriad of suburbs and bedroom communities. For many it's the only bookstore they have ever known.

Bookstores have become go-to hot spots for readings and other literary events, but Dallas-run reading series aren't all brand new. Arts & Letters Live, hosted at the Dallas Museum of Art, is a literary and performing arts series that has brought in big audiences to see award-winning authors and poets since 1992. Participants have included Margaret Atwood, David

Sedaris, Sandra Cisneros, and many other high-profile literary names. The Pegasus Reading Series, curated by poet Sebastian Paramo and Courtney Marie of Spiderweb Salon and often hosted by Kettle Art Gallery in Deep Ellum, showcases local and touring poets and writers. The Authors Live! series co-sponsored by Friends of the SMU Libraries, Highland Park United Methodist Church, Friends of the Highland Park Library, and HPISD Parent Education Committee is celebrating its fifteenth year of showcasing award-winning authors from the state and nation.

Besides bookstores and reading series, events and avenues for literary experiences include DaVerse Lounge, through Life in Deep Ellum, featuring open-mic spoken word and performance art. There's also Pandora's Box, a poetry showcase held at the historic Margo Jones Theater in Fair Park. The Writer's Garret is a literary center that features programming, education, and outreach; WordSpace was founded back in 1994 to connect talent with local audiences.

Authors in the Big D

Nationally known authors either living in the greater Dallas area or with Dallas connections include **Ben Fountain, Merritt Tierce, Kathleen Kent, Harry Hunsicker, Joe Milazzo, Sanderia Faye, Sebastian Paramo, Will Clarke, Luke Goebel, Joaquin Zihautanego, LaToya Watkins, Charlaine Harris, Rachel Caine, Julie Murphy,** and **Kellie Coates Gilbert,** among others.

Fiction and festivals

You may have heard of the literary magazine Carve, but did you know it was based in Dallas? Carve has been publishing fiction online and hosting the Raymond Carver Short Story Contest since 2000. The organization has since grown to include Carve Literary Services and Carve in the Classroom under its umbrella. Carve is a member of CLMP and attends the annual AWP conference.

Founded in 2006, the Dallas International Book Fair presented annual literary events showcasing works by internationally acclaimed authors as well as national, regional and local authors representing diverse regions of the world. This family event included artistic and cultural performances, film and book presentations, educational workshops and children's activities. The event was renamed in February 2014 as the Dallas Book Festival with a purpose to continue the goal of promoting a love for books, reading and literacy through multilingual and multicultural activities with a focus on spotlighting the city of Dallas and its wide range of ethnic and cultural diversity. This year's event will be Saturday, April 30 at the J. Erik Jonsson Central Library.

Other book festivals include: the SMU Literary Festival, which is known for bringing in rising literary stars and occurs the third week of March. The 20th annual Highland Park Literary Festival was held in February and brought in Dave Eggers, author and founder of *McSweeney's.*

Tulisoma South Dallas Book Fair, with its primary focus on Dallas's African-American community, occurs each August. "Tulisoma," Swahili for "we read," is a community-based festival promoting literacy and the arts in the South Dallas/Fair Park area. Founded in 2003 by the late **Leo V. Chaney, Jr.,** and **Dr. Harry Robinson,** president and CEO of the African American Museum, the goal of Tulisoma is to create a dynamic event tailored to engage local families, avid readers, aspiring writers and visitors to the city. The Dallas Public Library serves as the lead partner along with many community supporters and sponsors to continue the tradition of celebrating reading and the importance of literacy.

Reading, libraries, and literacy

Dallas doesn't do anything halfway. Many cities have a one city, one book program to encourage the citizenry to literally all get on the same page. But in 2015, the Dallas Public Library and Friends of the Library asked everyone to read Charles Portis's ***True***

Grit as part of D Academy's literacy nonprofit Big D Reads. D Academy fellows raised enough money to purchase 17,000 copies of the book and handed them out at more than 60 events during April 2015.

More destinations for your visit

For a generation Dallas has been notoriously linked with books—as in the Texas School Book Depository. Constructed in 1901, the red brick building on the corner of Houston and Elm streets was known as the Texas School Book Depository at the time of the assassination of President John F. Kennedy. The private firm stocked and distributed textbooks for public schools in north Texas and parts of Oklahoma.

Following the Kennedy assassination, the building became the focus of shock, grief and outrage. Evidence was found showing that shots were fired from the sixth floor, and Depository employee Lee Harvey Oswald was charged with the president's murder.

After the Texas School Book Depository Company moved out in 1970, some hoped the building would be torn down. It remained a painful reminder of what happened in 1963.

Dallas County acquired the building in 1977 with plans to locate county offices on the first five floors. After a major renovation, the Dallas County Administration Building was dedicated on March 29, 1981. The top two floors of the building, including the infamous sixth floor, remained empty.

On President's Day 1989, the Sixth Floor Museum opened as a response to the many visitors who come to Dealey Plaza to learn more about the assassination. The historical exhibition on the sixth floor highlights the impact of Kennedy's death on the nation and the world. Two key evidentiary areas on the sixth floor have been restored to their 1963 appearance.

On President's Day 2002, the museum opened the seventh floor gallery. This flexible space now provides an additional 5,500 square feet for innovative exhibitions, special events and public programming.

In July 2010, the museum opened the Reading Room—a reflective environment for anyone seeking information and understanding about the assassination and legacy of President John F. Kennedy. The Reading Room directly overlooks Dealey Plaza and provides researchers, educators and students with access to an extensive library which includes books, magazines and newspapers and covers topics ranging from Kennedy's life and legacy to conspiracy theories and 1960s pop culture.

Plan your visit

For more information on lodging, eats & drinks, and other visitor information, go to VisitDallas.com. To learn more about the area's history, visit the Texas Lakes Trail Region website.

TOP BOOKISH DESTINATION #4

Prettiest town we've ever seen — and one of the most literary, now that it's been proclaimed the Storybook Capital of Texas.

Abilene

SONGWRITER BOB GIBSON had never laid eyes on Abilene, Texas, when he immortalized the city in 1956 as the "prettiest town I've ever seen." Today Abilene celebrates that ditty, and a great cultural legacy that includes some of Texas's strongest journalist-authors; a long-running regional book festival; a university press; and a vibrant historic downtown with museums, galleries, library, book and gift stores; and a national center for illustrated children's books.

Lighting up downtown with Storybook Sculptures

The 84th Texas Legislature proclaimed Abilene the official **Storybook Capital of Texas.** The historic West Texas railroad city is home to such attractions and events as the National Center for Children's Illustrated

Literature, the Storybook Sculpture Project (thought to be the largest public collection of storybook sculptures in any city), and the annual Children's Art & Literacy Festival.

The heart of the city's downtown is a collection of seventeen outdoor statues that celebrate children's literature, including six bronze sculptures of beloved Dr. Seuss characters created by renowned artist Leo Rijn (Abilene is one of only a few cities in the nation to permanently exhibit these six iconic sculptures). In March 2016 the city, its civic organizers, and its downtown businesses and property owners took a major leap forward in coming together to support their literary heritage by lighting the sculptures at night. Downtown businesses and property owners will be maintaining the energy costs of fifty illuminations—including sculptures and trees. The illumination project was designed by a former lighting director for Disney.

The National Center for Children's Illustrated Literature (NCCIL) (above, submitted photo), known locally as "the Nickel," was founded in 1997 to honor the artwork of children's illustrators. It has since featured the works of award-winning children's books illustrators and authors, like **Dr. Seuss**, *Berenstain Bears* authors **Stan, Jan, and Michael Berenstain,** and **David Shannon.** In addition is has more than 150 pieces of original illustrations. The museum collaborates with award-winning artists to produce exhibitions of their artwork that are distinctive and appealing to visitors of all ages. In addition to this unique artistic partnership, following its debut at the NCCIL gallery, each exhibition travels to museums, public libraries, and galleries nationwide.

Each June the Children's Art & Literacy Festival (CALF) rocks the town in a downtown-wide event featuring the nationally recognized children's illustrator exhibiting that summer at the NCCIL. CALF showcases children's books through a parade, costume contests, readings, talks, and crafts. All events are based on the work of the featured CALF illustrator. New sculptures are dedicated during the festival.

Also while you're in downtown ...

Monk's Coffee Shop on Abilene's Cypress Street welcomes a slightly older literary crowd as they host open mic nights every Thursday for spoken word and singer-songwriter enthusiasts. Monk's supports arts of all stripes, with local paintings and drawings adorning their walls, and special open mic nights held in conjunction with Abilene's monthly Art Walk of galleries, museums, and studios.

The Grace Museum has hosted poetry workshops and literary experiences for visitors of all ages. A 55,000-square-foot museum housed in the former Hotel Grace built in 1909 by Col. W. L. Beckham of Greenville, Texas, is located at the corner of Cypress Street and North First Street. The Prairie Style hotel was initially a three-story structure, a fourth story was added in the late 1920s. A subsequent renovation removed the main portico, bricked up several main story windows and changed the hotel's name to the Drake Hotel. The Drake Hotel eventually ceased operation and fell into disrepair. The Abilene Preservation League and the Abilene Fine Arts Museum banded together in the late 1980s to save the neglected structure and provide a new and improved home for the Abilene Fine Arts Museum. Following major restoration in the early 1990s, the structure was placed on the National Register of Historic Places and opened to the public as the Museums of Abilene in 1992. Since 1992, the museum has existed as The Museums of Abilene, Grace Cultural Center and the name was officially changed to The Grace Museum in 1998.

Festivals and authors

This fall the West Texas Book Festival, sponsored by the Abilene Public Library and the Abilene Reporter-News, will mark its sixteenth anniversary with a five-day extravaganza featuring some of the state's favorite authors in a variety of genres. Abilene's event gives local and regional writers their turn in the spotlight as well, cultivating new careers and rising stars.

Each year the festival also presents the A. C. Greene Award to a distinguished Texas author for lifetime achievement. Native Abilenean **A. C. Greene** (1923-2002), known as the Dean of Texas Letters, was a columnist and editor for the *Abilene Reporter-News,* the *Dallas Times Herald,* and the *Dallas Morning News* who also earned fame as author, teacher, bookstore owner, musician, poet, and radio and television talk show host. Greene is best known for his numerous books and articles, both fiction and nonfiction, about or set in Texas—and for his early bibliography of de rigeur Lone Star reading, *Fifty Best Texas Books.*

Another pair of *Reporter-News* veterans, **Glenn Dromgoole** and **Carlton Stowers,** picked up Greene's mantle again with *101 Essential Texas Books* (ACU Press, 2014). Stowers, a 1960 Abilene High School graduate who also served as longtime Dallas Cowboys beat writer for the Dallas Morning News, is most noted for his true-crime books; he is a member of the Texas Institute of Letters and the Texas Literary Hall of Fame and also a recipient of the A. C. Greene Award.

Dromgoole writes the syndicated book column «Texas Reads» for this publication and several Texas daily newspapers and is the author of twenty-seven books and counting.

With his wife, Carol, Dromgoole has since 2004 run the Texas Star Trading Company, an independent bookstore and gift shop they playfully dub the National Store of Texas. You can't miss its storefront on historic Cypress Street, where the Lone Star flags fly gracefully in the West Texas breeze

The Dromgooles have both played an active role in the West Texas Book Festival as well. Festival events are generally held at the **Abilene Public Library** at 2nd and Cedar Streets, and the Abilene Civic Center on North 6th.

In the spring, from March through May, the **Abilene Friends of the Library** host a monthly author series of leading Texas authors talking about their books.

Other authors from Abilene or with Abilene ties include **Stephen Harrigan,** Christian romance author **Karen Witemeyer,** poet **Robert A. Fink,** children's author **Penny Parker Klosterman,** and the father-daughter duo **Joe Specht** and **Mary Helen Specht.**

Publishing and book craft
Abilene Christian University Press, the publishing arm of one of Abilene's three religious denominational universities (the others are McMurry and Hardin-

Simmons), produces books about Texas culture and history as well as theological volumes and textbooks. ACU Press has kept the stories of its home city alive with **Glenn Dromgoole** and **Jay Moore's** *Abilene A to Z* (2015), **Moore's** *Abilene in Plain Sight* (2014) and **Dromgoole, Moore,** and **Joe Specht's** *Abilene Stories: From Then to Now* (2013).

At H. V. Chapman and Sons (above) on North 3rd Street, Tim de la Vega and his team of about a dozen carry on the family tradition of book and Bible binding and conservation begun here by Stan Chapman in 1947. De la Vega, himself a product of a multi-generational printing family, feels called to this work like a mission -- and his staff share that passion for books. Though they have integrated digital and offset printing into the mix these days and, according to business development manager Jody Rood, are looking to grow and fine-tune their operations, the firm earns its loyal following through the ancient craft of the book bindery. Here is the domain of the letterpress, the stamping foil, the book press, and all the arcane tools thereof. Besides its business serving local organizations with custom print runs and stamping the Bibles used in the state capitol, HVC bound some 25,000 books last year the old-school way. Stop by and say hello — HVC's current location is a fine example of historic preservation and adaptive reuse, and the old building's a veritable museum and archive as well.

And while you're in the area ...

Frontier Texas tells the story of the region in multimedia form. Drawing from history and texts of West Texas's Native American, ranching, and settlement roots, the museum brings the Old West to life with the help of state-of-the-art technology. Frontier Texas also serves as the official visitor center for Abilene and the Texas Forts Trail Region, and it has an excellent bookstore onsite to boot.

No visit to the Abilene area is complete without a visit to historic Buffalo Gap Village and a culinary destination of statewide merit—**Perini Ranch Steakhouse,** where you can pick up a copy of the illustrated Texas Cowboy Cooking to try some of steakmaster Tom Perini's mouth-watering recipes long after you've returned home. The Perini Ranch also sports two guesthouses on the property with a peaceful and tranquil setting in the middle of the wooded ranch land—a great venue for a writer's—or reader's retreat.

Plan your visit

The city's Convention and Visitor Bureau can help you plan your visit to the area, with excellent lodging, dining, and recreation recommendations. Find them at www.AbileneVisitors.com. To learn more about the area's history, visit the Texas Forts Trail Region website.

Above: Texas Star Trading Company, Cypress Street

TOP BOOKISH DESTINATION #5

Midland and Odessa may seem far from the big-city lights of Dallas, Houston, and Austin, but both cities celebrate the literary arts in unique ways.

Permian Basin: Midland-Odessa

Ratliff Stadium, THE HOME of Odessa's Permian Panthers, familiarly known as Mojo, has been called one of the nation's ten must-see high school football venues. Built in 1982 at a cost of $5.6 million, the 19,302-seat stadium figures prominently in the chronicle of a year in the life of a team—*Friday Night Lights* by Philadelphia sportswriter **Buzz Bissinger.**

Nostalgia was running high for Mojo last year as author Bissinger released the 25th anniversary edition of the famous book. In this latest update Bissinger revisited many of the high school football players, now middle-aged men, and he returned to the Permian Basin with his book tour. Famously, when his title was released in the 1980s, some considered it an exposé, and Bissinger was not exactly a popular figure in Odessa for a while. But through the movie, the TV series, and several editions of the FNL books, locals have mellowed in their responses to their literary and screen fame. It›s no exaggeration to say that Bissinger›s book has been a factor in the ranking of Odessa a Texas bookish destination.

This fall Ratliff Stadium will be the setting for a new era in football in Odessa. **The University of Texas of the Permian Basin** is bringing college football to its hometown and will play in the historic venue. In addition to the passion that Odessa has had for Friday Night Lights, it will now have the opportunity to exert that enthusiasm on Saturday afternoons. UTPB has raised more than $9 million to add a football program that will begin play in the 2016 season, with the Falcons joining NCAA Division II's Lone Star Conference. The effort to bring football to UTPB was launched in order to help increase the school's student enrollment from its current 5,500 to around 8,000 by 2022.

Another academic institution, **Odessa College**, is played host to the Permian Basin's biggest literary event in April 2016—Books in the Basin. The Odessa Council for the Arts and the Humanities, Odessa College, and the Friends of the Ector County Library will host more than forty authors from across the country, state, and region. Featured authors include **Lev Grossman** (SyFy's *The Magicians*), **Judd Winick** (*Hilo*), **Alfredo Corchado** (*Midnight in Mexico*), The Cooking Channel's **The Fabulous Beekman Boys**, **Sandra Brown** (*Friction*), and **Jodi Thomas** (*Rustler's Moon*). Special events included a Writer's League of Texas session and the return of Literary Death Match to West Texas.

In fall 2016, the **Permian Basin Writers' Workshop** will return to Midland, focusing on the craft and business of writing. The 2015 event brought literary agent, author, and native son **Seth Fishman** and Stanton native **Stephen Graham Jones**, among others, to the award-winning Midland Centennial Library to share their wisdom.

Midland's Library

Crowds stood in line for the grand opening of the state-of-the-art Centennial Library in Midland (below; contributed photo) in 2013. Former first lady **Laura Bush**, author of a memoir, *Spoken from the Heart*, and Gen. Tommy Franks, author of a memoir, *American Soldier*, were on hand for the ribbon cutting. Franks attended Midland High School and graduated from Robert E. Lee High School, one year ahead of Mrs. Bush.

By November of that year *Library Journal* had named Centennial one of its Destination Places, describing how it was "transformed from a stand-alone retail facility, the best case of 'adaptive reuse.' Among the high-tech amenities in the nearly $8 million building are dedicated children's and teen spaces featuring an interactive work wall and an interactive floor. The library also includes a media lab, movable walls and partitions, and a variety of seating options."

The following year **John Trischitti III,** who goes by Mr. T in his ongoing community outreach efforts using YouTube, Twitter, Facebook, Pinterest, and other social media, was named Texas Librarian of the Year.

A home of presidents—and books

Across town on West Ohio is another literary destination. At the George W. Bush Childhood Home in Midland, children get a free book each day that they visit. There are also many reading events and a leave-a-book option as well. The 43rd president himself has authored a memoir, *Decision Points*.

Literary Midland

A must-visit destination for book lovers —and lovers of Southwestern history—is the Haley Memorial Library and History Center (below) on Indiana Avenue, near the Museum of the Southwest complex. The research library, archive, and art collection are open daily to visitors and researchers.

Current Midland authors include **Patrick Dearen**, nominated by the Western Writers of America for a Spur award for his most recent novel, *The Big Drift*. **Laura Drake** was the 2014 RITA award winner from the Romance Writers of America for Best First Book, for *The Sweet Spot*. Another of Dearen's books is *Halff of Texas: Merchant Rancher of the Old West*, a biography of Mayer Halff, who owned or leased several ranches, including the huge Quien Sabe Ranch, which would encompass five to six hundred square miles across Midland and Glasscock counties.

Odessa's museums and more

The Ellen Noël Art Museum of the Permian Basin, located near the UTPB campus, is a destination that supports reading and literary initiatives in a variety of ways—including a little free library and story time with interactive art activities for youngsters.

Two other museums near the UTPB campus should also be on any literary/political traveler's list when visiting Odessa — The John Ben Shepperd Public Leadership Institute and the Presidential Museum.

John Ben Shepperd spent his life describing with great clarity the value of public service, mutual respect, ethics, and public leadership. Lieutenant Governor Bob Bullock created the institute in 1995 to honor those values and provide a mechanism for educating young Texans about them. The Shepherd Leadership Institute often hosts nationally known authors and pundits in special programs, lectures, and discussions on the meaning of public service.

Odessa's Presidential Museum and Leadership Library is an exceptional repository for presidential portraits, documents, campaign memorabilia, signatures and collectibles that represent each of the country's presi-

A Guide to the State's Top Bookish Destinations 51

dents. The museum was conceived as a memorial to the highest office in the land shortly after the assassination of John F. Kennedy in 1963. Today it has an outstanding collection of one of a kind exhibits that tell the history of the office in a dramatic, memorable way. Also included at the museum are artifacts of the nation's first ladies, vice presidents, and presidential candidates, as well as presidents of the Republic of Texas and the Confederate States of America.

The **Odessa College** campus is home to a site (and sight) that surprises many travelers: the most authentic permanent replica of London's original 1598 Globe Theater (below), along with a to-scale replica of Stratford-upon-Avon's Anne Hathaway Cottage. Visitors may tour the complex and enjoy performances of Shakespeare's works and other dramas, year-round. Visit the website of the Globe of the Great Southwest for schedules and info.

Authors who call Odessa home or who have connections to Odessa include romance author **Ann Swann** and true crime writer **Glen Aaron.**

Plan your visit

Midland and Odessa each have well-staffed Convention and Visitor Bureaus to help you plan your visit to the area, with excellent lodging, dining, and recreation recommendations. Find them at www.VisitMidland.com and www.OdessaCVB.com. To learn more about the area's history, visit the Texas Pecos Trail Region website.

TOP BOOKISH DESTINATION #6

The Alamo City hosts the state's largest spring book festival, celebrates 40 years of pioneer Wings Press, and welcomes readers to the Twig's new digs in the rehabbed Pearl Brewery complex.

San Antonio

A GREAT DEAL OF WHAT MAKES ANY PLACE a bookish destination is the presence of a resident literary sage who's readily accessible to like-minded seekers. For San Antonio, that spirit is **Bryce Milligan**, publisher, writer, and all-around man of letters whose pathbreaking Wings Press celebrated its fortieth anniversary in November 2015.

The San Antonio Current, looking back at Wings's history and Milligan's two decades at its helm, described him as "a literary godfather in this community."

A visitor might cross paths with Milligan and his writer/librarian wife, **Mary Guererro Milligan,** at San Antonio hangouts like Gemini Ink or the eye-popping public library, which hosted an exhibition of Wings Press work last fall. "Perhaps the best part about Milligan and Wings," wrote James Courtney in the Current, "is that they have consistently sought to publish work by writers who are underrepresented in published literature and to work with Texas writers whose works, in various ways, preserve our diverse cultural heritage."

THE CORAZÓN OF AMERICAN SMALL PRESS PUBLISHING

Crossroads of culture, fertile soil for writers

San Antonio, as the birthplace of the Texas Republic and a cultural crossroads for centuries before that, beats today as the heart of Texas's multicultural literary life. With guest reading series and appearances at the city's institutions from the **University of Texas at San Antonio** to **Our Lady of the Lake University, University of the Incarnate Word,** and **St. Mary›s University**—to name only a few—the city offers rich and regular opportunities for listening and interacting.

Latina author and MacArthur "genius grant" winner **Sandra Cisneros** has for three decades been most closely associated with her adopted hometown of San Antonio—as much for her championship of Latino/a culture here as the ways she captured Tejano life in works such as ***Woman Hollering Creek and Other***

Stories and the novel ***Caramelo.*** After finding first fame with ***The House on Mango Street,*** set in her native Chicago but published by Houston-based Arte Público Press in 1984, she established the Macondo Workshops to build community and social change through art and writing. The workshops, and the Macondo Foundation, continue today under the local Guadalupe Cultural Arts Center. Cisneros's once-controversial purple-painted house (now a more sedate rose color), at 735 Guenther St. in the King William Historic District, sold in January 2015 some while after the author's long-announced move to Mexico. Cisneros's work figures prominently in the 2015 anthology ***Her Texas,*** only one acknowledgment of the influence this author and state have exercised over one another.

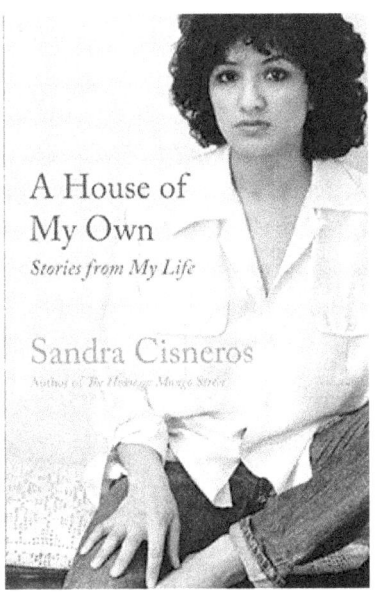

Another writer from San Antonio's past honed his craft in the Alamo City more than 130 years ago—short-story master and temporary Texan **William Sidney Porter,** later and better known by the pseudonym **O. Henry**. The North Carolina native, who came with his father to a friend's Texas ranch in 1882 and spent a year writing and publishing a humor rag in a two-room German stone house on San Antonio's Presa Street in 1885, drew deeply on his varied experiences in the Lone Star State (read more under Austin). Today you can visit the tiny house, relocated along with its Texas historical marker to the corner of Laredo and Dolorosa Streets, where O. Henry first published ***The Rolling Stone.***

Other renowned writers past and present are connected with the city, which one pundit claimed in 2009 "would never be known as a book town."* Author **Stephen Harrigan** captured the drama of San Antonio's most renowned landmark in his best-selling historical novel ***The Gates of the Alamo*** (he's written books set in several of this year's Top Ten cities, too, including Houston, the Austin area, San Antonio, and Abilene). *The Gates of the Alamo* was honored in 2001 with the TCU Texas Book Award, the Western Heritage Award from the National Cowboy and Western Heritage Museum, and the Spur Award for Best Novel of the West.

San Antonio restaurateur **Cappy Lawton** and writer **Chris Waters Dunn** in 2015 published a veritable encyclopedia of a local culinary staple in ***Enchiladas:***

Aztec to Tex-Mex, gorgeously designed and illustrated as well as filled with recipes and food history.

San Antonio author (and native of the oil-patch town of Wink) **Leila Meacham** proves it's never too late to pursue your writing dreams. Her novel *Roses,* often described as a Texas *Gone With the Wind,* was published in 2010 when the author was 65 and has now sold more than a million copies. Meacham followed it up with *Tumbleweeds* and *Somerset,* also Texas bestsellers, and *Titans* is slated for a spring 2016 release.

Other authors living and working in San Antonio include 2016 Texas poet laureate (and 2014–16 city of San Antonio poet laureate) **Laurie Ann Guerrero; Nan Cuba (*Body and Bread*)**, novelist/playwright/screenwriter **Bill Sibley,** novelist **James R. Dennis** (one-third of the writing team that goes by **Miles Arceneaux**), and fiction writer **Andrew Porter. Rick Riordan** (*The Lightning Thief*) formerly called San Antonio home; poets **Gregg Barrios, Naomi Shihab Nye,** and **Carmen Tafolla** still do.

Bookstores and more

Rosengren's Books: An Oasis for Mind and Spirit by *Mary Carolyn Hollers George,* released January 2015 by Wings Press archives the cultural impact of the legendary San Antonio bookstore. Rosengren›s was the center of literary culture not only in San Antonio, but in Texas, for decades. The late **Willie Morris,** the respected author and editor of *Harper's* magazine, called it "one of the finest and most admirable bookstores in America." To **Robert**

Frost, it was simply "the best of bookstores." Writers as diverse as **J. Frank Dobie, John Dos Passos, John Graves,** and **Larry McMurtry** simply loved the place.

The Twig (below) today carries on the independent bookstore tradition at The Pearl, the shopping and arts district created from the old Pearl Brewery. Other bookstores include Nine Lives (used books) and Imagine Books and Records.

Greater San Antonio also boasts five Barnes & Noble stores, three Half Price Books, and a Books-a-Million. The city's many world-class museums, including those at the Alamo, the Witte Museum, the Institute of Texan Cultures, and the Briscoe Western Art Museum, carry extensive selections of books in their museum stores as well.

Publishing flourishes here. In addition to Wings Press, which the Bloomsbury Review called "The best little publishing house in Texas," Trinity University Press, now under the direction of **Tom Payton,** publishes authors such as cultural historian **Rebecca Solnit,** National Book Award–winning writer **Barry**

Lopez (who also does a regular stint as visiting writer at Texas Tech in Lubbock) and Pulitzer Prize–winning poet **W. S. Merwin.** In December 2014 Trinity acquired the assets of Maverick Publishing Company, founded by San Antonio historian, author, and former newspaperman **Lewis F. Fisher,** and announced plans to launch a new imprint, Maverick Books, in early 2015 which will include backlist of the original Maverick line while building a larger list of titles committed to the history and culture of Texas and the American Southwest.

In a city known for its colorful arts culture, book arts thrive as well. At the Southwest School of Art, the Paper and Book Arts Department offers both traditional and explorative classes at all levels in papermaking, bookbinding, decorative paper techniques and letterpress printing. Papermaking and Book Arts classes are held in the Picante Paper and Book Arts Studios located on the second floor of the Navarro Campus.

Spoken word in San Antonio includes **PuroSlam,** the only nationally certified poetry slam operating in the city. Started in 1999 by Benjamin Ortiz, PuroSlam has earned a national reputation as one of the toughest, roughest, rowdiest poetry slams in the United States, bringing the exciting world of performance poetry to South Texas on a weekly basis. Gemini Ink, also home to a vibrant spoken word series, brings writers and readers together at 1111 Navarro Street.

San Antonio Book Festival

The San Antonio Book Festival {above), the city's annual literary extravaganza, takes place in early April at the Central Library and Southwest School of Art.

The festival is presented by, and benefits, the San Antonio Public Library, a system comprising a central library and twenty-four branches. The six-story, 240,000-square-foot Central Library building at 600 Soledad, opened in 1995, is easily recognized by its bright-colored, striking "Mexican Modernist" design and its "Enchilada Red" color.

Plan your visit

The city's Convention and Visitor Bureau can help you plan your visit to the area, with excellent lodging, dining, and recreation recommendations. Find them at www.VisitSanAntonio.com. To learn more about the area's history, visit the Texas Independence Trail Region website.

A Guide to the State's Top Bookish Destinations 61

TOP BOOKISH DESTINATION #7

It's where the West begins, and where your search for great libraries, bookstores, and events ends. While you're visiting the Stockyards, spend a little time reading up, too

Fort Worth

YOUR LOCAL NEWSPAPER has been called The Daily Miracle. It's a place where writers, artists, salespeople, and number crunchers come together and create news coverage from scratch every day. Since 1995 and the digital era, it's been a 24/7 miracle.

The ***Fort Worth Star-Telegram*** came of age in the early twentieth century, when larger-than-life men such as **Amon G. Carter, William Randolph Hearst,** and **Joseph Pulitzer** acquired newspapers and newspaper readers through aggressive beat reporting instead of hostile takeovers by shareholders agitating for better portfolio performance. Texas's daily newspapers have also served as a quasi-book boot camp for a generation of aspiring authors.

The Fort Worth journalism scene has proven fertile ground for authors such as **Gary Cartwright, Dan Jenkins, Bud Shrake, Molly Ivins, Sandra Brown, Jeff Guinn,** and **Julia Heaberlin.** These authors have generated best sellers on the national scene over recent decades.

Not all of Fort Worth's literary talent originated in the newsroom, however. Fans of the late **Patricia Highsmith** may recall that she was born in Fort Worth in 1921. Folklorist and historian **Joyce Gibson Roach,** who captures the experience of ranch women in the

Southwest, taught for many years in Fort Worth and ranches in nearby Wise County. **J'Nell Pate,** author of several volumes of Fort Worth history and now retired from Tarrant Community College, has contributed a western history column to her hometown paper every week since (yes, you read this right) 1968.

A leader in regional letters based in Fort Worth, **Texas Christian University Press** has traditionally published the history and literature of Texas and the American West, including the Literary Texas Cities book series founded by former director (and now novelist) **Judy Alter.** (Part literary history, part anthology, these samplers are still available in print or used.)

As the press has grown steadily in stature and in its ability to bring credit to its parent university over the last twenty years, it has been praised for its regional fiction, which often doesn't find a market in New York, and for discovering and preserving local history.

TCU Press has several established series and some new ones. The Texas Tradition Series reprints classic Texas literature that might otherwise disappear from bookstores and libraries—with novelist **Elmer Kelton** as its mainstay. The Chisholm Trail Series offers books that capture the history and culture of Texas, and Chaparral Books for Young Readers are historical fiction for middle-school students.

In Western literature, ***The Big Drift*** (2014) by **Patrick Dearen** won the Western Writers of America 2015 Spur Award.

The Texas Biography Series, sponsored by the Center for Texas Studies at TCU, offers scholarly, documented biographies of lesser-known Texans—Sam Houston and Stephen F. Austin have been covered extensively, but many who made strong contributions to Texas history have not. The first volume, *Emily Austin of Texas: 1795–1851,* by **Light T. Cummins,** won the 2010 Liz Carpenter Award for Research in the History of Women.

Poetry and poets laureate

TCU Press is also home to the Texas Poets Laureate series, books collecting recent and new work by the Texas poets laureate beginning with **Alan Birkelbach,** 2005, through **Karla K. Morton,** 2010 Texas poet laureate.

Speaking of poets, the Fort Worth Poetry Society, which recently celebrated its 105th anniversary, is the longest active poetry society in Texas.

Writing on the frontier

Fort Worth's been called the place where the west begins, and that frontier spirit contributes to the name of its most popular and still evolving literary/cultural festival, the Wildcatter's Exchange, described by organizers as "Two Days of Rhythm & Rhymes, Truth & Lies." The Wildcatter Exchange's third annual, two-day free festival is slated for Friday and Saturday, March 25-26, 2016, in Fort Worth's South Main Village District. The focus of this year's festival will be a musical, historical, and dramatic survey of Fort

Worth's I. M. Terrell High School and the influence of its jazz-study programs upon the popular music industry worldwide. Featured authors include **Joe R. Lansdale, Ron Abrahm**, and **Drew Sanders**.

Fort Worth's fifth annual Art & Words Show (above; submitted photo), curated by author **Bonnie Jo Stufflebeam** with guest editor **Jenn Aglio,** will take place on Saturday, October 1, 2016; the show starts at 6:30 pm and the reading at 7:30. To submit work for consideration, and learn more about this multimedia event, visit its website.

Libraries, bookstores, and history

Turn to another chapter of revisiting Fort Worth's history at the Fort Worth Public Library. They devote the entire month of June to local history, with special events and readings that they take to the streets—literally—with the Fort Worth History Bike Tour. In June 2016 FWPL is offering library card holders a chance to pedal their way to historic downtown buildings with Cowtown Cycle Party with guide Rick Selcer (the event is limited to ages 18 and up, with limited seating and reservations required).

The Fort Worth Library offers an extensive variety of literary-related events, calendars and community outreach year-round. Fort Worth also famously hosts the Texas Literary Hall of Fame. Founded by the Friends of the Library in 2004, the Texas Literary Hall of Fame honors authors whose body of work enhances Texas' literary heritage, is original and first published in this country, and has already been recognized for its literary significance. Held biennially, the Hall of Fame is commemorated by the "Texas Tales" painting by Marjorie Stark Buckley hanging in the west wing of the Central Library.

For readers who'd rather own their books than borrow them, Fort Worth boasts more than a dozen new and used bookstores, including Monkey and Dog Books, a children's bookshop that hosts events throughout the year and a storytime every Wednesday and Thursday at 10:30 a.m. The library is also hosts the Worth Reading Series, bringing many visiting writers to the city.

Fort Worth is also home to the Dock Bookshop, the largest independent, full service, African-American owned bookstore in Texas and the Southwest, which opened in 2008. The Dock hosts a long-running Poetry & Open Mic Tuesday nights at 8:00.

Located in greater Fort Worth are four **Barnes & Nobles,** three **Mardel** Christian book stores, three **Half Price Books** stores, and a **Books-a-Million.** And since this issue was published online in spring 2016, we heard the news that entrepreneur and author Paul Combs is opening a new indie bookstore in the Southside neighborhood, calling it The Last Word. Combs says the store will also feature a book club; the inaugural theme will be "Around the World in 80 Books."

Museums and more

Fort Worth's extensive array of world-class museums have a variety of unique books to purchase as well, and considering that many of the local museums will be featuring exhibits and events related to books in 2016, that should be easy to achieve as you take in their offerings. Perhaps one of the most notable of Fort Worth events is the twenty-fifth anniversary exhibition of **Larry McMurtry's *Lonesome Dove,*** with portions at both the Sid Richardson Museum and the Cowgirl Hall of Fame.

"Lonesome Dove: The Art of Story" runs through June 19 and traces the path of this quintessential Texas work from McMurtry's Pulitzer Prize-winning novel to the original screenplay and filming of the legendary TV miniseries.

The Sid Richardson Museum is the trailhead, kicking off the multifaceted January-through-June citywide celebration, The Lonesome Dove Reunion and Trail. The Trail includes exhibitions at four museums, along with screenings, seminars, and a reunion gala of the cast and crew of the award-winning 1989 TV miniseries with luminaries Robert Duvall (who portrayed character Gus McCrae), Tommy Lee Jones (who portrayed Woodrow Call), Diane Lane, Anjelica Huston, and others.

At the Modern Art Museum visitors can view the monumental Anselm Kiefer sculpture "Book with Wings," or stroll the **Trinity Trails** park area to view sculptures representing a wide range of literary history — from **Mark Twain** reading a book, to **Dr. Seuss** figures.

Plan your visit

The city's Convention and Visitor Bureau can help you plan your visit to the area, with excellent lodging, dining, and recreation recommendations. Find them at www.FortWorth.com. To learn more about the area's history, visit the TexasLakesTrail Region website.

TOP BOOKISH DESTINATION #8

Far West Texas is a bilingual, bicultural literary mecca, home to Benjamin Alire Sáenz and dozens of other working writers, the Cormac McCarthy legend, award-winning Cinco Puntos Press.

El Paso

EL PASO IS A LITERARY DESTINATION where borders, parameters, and limits are superfluous as residents, readers, and writers cross the boundaries seamlessly between two states, two countries, and two languages. Differences like genre and written versus spoken word seem easily surmountable as well.

Perhaps the first book to capture the absence of convention for border locales like El Paso was Texas author and critic Gloria E. Anzaldúa's Borderlands/La Frontera: The New Mestiza (1987) a semi-autobiographical work that treated the invisible "borders" that exist between Latinas/os and non-Latinas/os, men and women, heterosexuals and homosexuals, and numerous other opposing groups.

This Texas tradition of groundbreaking literature continues today, widely supported in individual literary pursuits and group gatherings at the University of Texas El Paso. UTEP brings an international celebration of language and the book arts routinely to its campus with gatherings such as the XXI Undécimo Congreso de Literatura Mexicana Contemporánea, the recent 2016 Contemporary Mexican Literature Conference, organized by the UTEP Department of Languages and Linguistics.

UTEP faculty include such literary luminaries as **Benjamín Alire Sáenz,** the first Latino writer ever to win the PEN/Faulkner award, and **Tim Z. Hernandez,** a poet, novelist, and performance artist whose collections of poetry *Skin Tax* (2005) and *Natural Takeover of Small Things* (University of Arizona Press, 2013) and novels *Breathing, In Dust* (Texas Tech University Press, 2009) and *Mañana Means Heaven* (University of Arizona Press, 2013) have garnered numerous international awards.

Sáenz's short-story collection that garnered the PEN/Faulkner (as well as a Lambda Literary Award in the Gay Fiction category),*Everything Begins and Ends at the Kentucky Club,* was published in 2012 by El Paso's own Cinco Puntos Press (below, contributed photo). Novelist and publisher **Lee Merrill Byrd** founded the publishing house in 1985 with her husband, poet **Bobby Byrd,** and named the enterprise after their El Paso neighborhood.

Readings, workshops, and more

Former El Pasoan **Pat Mora** is an award-winning poet and author of books for adults, teens, and children. Her awards include a poetry fellowship from the National Endowment for the Arts, a Golden Kite Award, and multiple American Library Association Notable Book awards, and honorary doctorates. A former teacher and university administrator, she is the founder of the family literacy initiative El día de los niños / El día de los libros, Children's Day / Book Day (Día). The year-long commitment to linking all children to books, languages, and cultures, and of sharing what Mora calls "book-joy," culminates in celebrations across the country in April. These days Mora lives in Santa Fe, New Mexico.

When writers and authors host a reading or signing in the El Paso area, they are just as apt to cross the border into New Mexico to Casa Camino Real in Las Cruces, the bookstore and gallery owned by **Denise Chavez,** a performance writer, novelist, and teacher who lives and works on the U.S.–Mexico border corridor in southern New Mexico. Her highly acclaimed books include, most recently, *The King and Queen of Comezón* (University of Oklahoma Press, 2014).

Poetry and the spoken word are vital currents in the El Paso scene. BorderSenses, a nonprofit literary organization, is devoted to promoting art and literature on both sides of the border through events like the **Barbed Wire Open Mic series,** which features performances in poetry, music, comedy, fiction, nonfiction, monologues, dance routines, and more. The Tumblewords Project and the **El Paso Poetry Project** also support poetry workshops and spoken-word performance workshops.

Publishing and book arts in El Paso

El Paso might seem an unlikely outpost of fine printing and book arts, but for decades during the long and varied career of Carl Hertzog, the "Printer at the Pass," it was the source of Texas's most prized and beautiful books. The papers of the designer-typographer-printer who taught at UTEP and founded the Texas Western Press are housed in the university's library. A lectureship named for Hertzog continues today via the Friends of the Library.

CARL HERTZOG
PRINTER
EL PASO TEXAS

In addition to the fine work turned out in El Paso by Cinco Puntos, El Paso–based **Mouthfeel Press** publishes and promotes poetry by new and established poets in the borderlands through an annual chapbook competition, anthologies, and community poetry readings.

Another independent press joined El Paso's literary scene in 2015. **Veliz Books** seeks quality and original literature from authors writing in English, Spanish, or Portuguese, and is also committed to publishing translations into English because they believe in cultivating artistic and literary connections that transcend geographical, cultural, and political borders. Their current catalog, at www.velizbooks.com, shows three authors.

Landscape and literature

Dramatic and desert landscapes have always defined El Paso. During most of the twentieth century the figure who best captured those landscapes, as well as scenes around the globe, was El Pasoan **Tom Lea,** also writer and illustrator of the bestselling novels *The Brave Bulls* and *The Wonderful Country* and numerous nonfiction works. Lea's extraordinary productions, from paintings to post office murals to stained glass to military cartoons, can be appreciated throughout the city. The El Paso Public Library Building is itself a mini-museum of contributions from renowned El Paso artists. One of the best vistas overlooking the cities of El Paso and Juarez, Mexico, is from **Tom Lea Park,** which you can reach by driving up East Schuster Avenue above El Paso High School.

In a more contemporary view of the region, photographer **Mark Paulda's** *El Paso 120* (TCU Press, 2014) goes beyond showcasing the scenery to make a powerful statement: "El Paso is not at the edge but instead at the very center of some remarkably amazing landscape." Paulda takes his audience on journeys to striking destinations within a 120-mile radius of the border city.

National Book Award winner and Rhode Island native **Cormac McCarthy** came to El Paso in the 1970s to write in "one of the last real cities left in America" and achieved both international renown a following intensely devoted to his distinctive prose But here he's always remembered as the writer who moved to the border and retreated from the limelight, eschewing signings, interviews, and lectures. The author of *Blood Meridian* (1985), *All the Pretty Horses* (1992), and *Cities on the Plain* (1999) bought a one-story adobe home on Coffin Avenue in suburban El Paso that later inspired author, painter, photographer, and actor-director **Peter Josyph** to pose provocative, unexpected questions in Cormac McCarthy's House about McCarthy's work, how it is achieved, and how it is interpreted. Sixty-five of Josyph's paintings of the house were exhibited in 1998 at the Centennial Museum in El Paso. Though McCarthy departed for New Mexico some years back, his legend thrives here.

El Paso supports two **Barnes & Noble** stores and is home to the **El Paso Writers League** and a chapter of **Sisters in Crime.** For an excellent selection of works by regional writers, drive down to the Bookery on the Mission Trail in Soccoro. It's worth the trip along the scenic route, but you just might be rewarded with the discovery of a book by **Sergio Troncoso, Sarah McCoy, Dagoberto Gilb, Rigoberto González, Leon Claire Metz, Estela Portillo Trambley,** or **Daniel Chacon** that will open the door to a new appreciation of El Paso.

Plan your visit

The city's Convention and Visitor Bureau can help you plan your visit to the area, with excellent lodging, dining, and recreation recommendations. Find them at www.VisitElPaso.com. To learn more about the area's history, visit the TexasMountainTrail Region website.

TOP BOOKISH DESTINATION #9

Denton's reputation as a destination for indie music and film also extends to its appeal for book lovers of all ages.

Denton

IT WOULD NOT BE HYPERBOLE to say that one book recently drew earth-shattering state and national attention to Denton, Texas—**Adam Briggle's** *A Field Philosopher's Guide to Fracking: How One Texas Town Stood Up to Big Oil and Gas* (October 2015). The UNT professor's book chronicles his—and his city's—odyssey to understand the economic and environmental impact of this controversial drilling technology.

Denton, the state, and the land have a storied history. A Texas land grant led to the formation of Denton County in 1846, and the city was incorporated in 1866, thus the Redbud Capital of Texas celebrates its sesquicentennial this year. The arrival of a railroad line in the city in 1881 spurred population, and the establishment of the **University of North Texas** in 1890 and **Texas Woman's University** in 1901. As of 2013 its population was 123,099, making it the eleventh largest city in the Dallas–Fort Worth metroplex area.

Located on the north end of the metroplex on Interstate 35, Denton is known for its active music life: the **North Texas State Fair and Rodeo,** the Denton Arts and Jazz Festival, and the **Denton Music Festival** attract more than 300,000 people to the city each year. With more than 45,000 students enrolled at the two universities located within its city limits, Denton (known around here as Little D) is often characterized as a college town, and its academia sows seeds of a rich literary culture.

A Literary Borough

Due in equal parts to the city's creative class and the University of North Texas's prestigious creative writing program, which yearly brings in around eight well-renowned writers as part of its Visiting Writers Series (past writers have included **Michael Ondaatje** (*The English Patient*), **Claire Vaye Watkins** (*Gold, Fame, Citrus*), and **Li-Young Li** (*The City in Which I Love You*), the *Ploughshares* journal included Denton in its list of "Literary Boroughs" a few years back.

UNT also hosts **University of North Texas Press,** the book publishing arm of the university that specializes in music, military history, Western, and environmental books and that hosts and publishes the winner of the annual Katherine Anne Porter Prize in Short Fiction and the annual Vassar Miller Prize in Poetry. UNT's Mayborn School of Journalism hosts the Mayborn

Literary Nonfiction Writers Conference (below, contributed photo). Denton is also home to the **Denton Poets' Assembly,** which has been meeting monthly since 2005.

The North Texas festival and reading scene

The North Texas Book Festival, a venue to sign/sell books published by their authors or by small or independent presses has occurred each spring in Denton since 2003. The funds that the NTBF raises through fees to authors for bookselling and contests goes to library grants.

Denton also boasts a robust underground literary community, with reading series popping up every year: Spiderweb Salon, a community of writers and artists of all stripes that hosts multiple themed and unthemed showcases per year, and the Kraken, a poetry series that brings in poets both local and global.

Since 1983 Denton's courthouse square has been home to the popular Recycled Books, a three-floor used bookstore in the old historic opera house.

Denton has also been the setting of many novels: **Lee Martin's** *Quakertown* and *Break the Skin* and **Carolyn Meyer's** *White Lilacs*. Science fiction writer **Darin Bradley's** *Noise* takes place in Denton.

Downtown Denton

The center of Denton's arts and humanities culture is its Downtown Square, with its mélange of music and food. But unless you're a local you wouldn't know. Behind the daily sounds that have become the norm of the Downtown Square there is another culture that lives among musicians and dining connoisseurs. If you decide to jump off of DART's Green Line at the Trinity Mills station and head north on the A-Train you may encounter some art illumination at various spots in Denton. Yes, Denton has its own metro rail, and there's much talk about Denton being the center of high-speed rail between Dallas and Houston in the next decade.

The **Denton Public Library** and its three branches embody the organization's mission statement: The Denton Public Library builds community by promoting lifelong learning, encouraging human connections and sharing resources.

Its services include The Forge, a technology makerspace at the library's North Branch that debuted in April 2014 and is available for use by individuals and groups of up to 20. The Forge contains various hardware options and specialized software for design and creative use as well as electronic components and 3D printing options. The Forge debuted in April 2014.

The library also hosts Spanish-language and English-language story times, provides bike repair workshops, and hosts a teenage cooking competition, along with yoga and chess classes.

Plan your visit

The city's Convention and Visitor Bureau can help you plan your visit to the area, with excellent lodging, dining, and recreation recommendations. Find them at www.DiscoverDenton.com. To learn more about the area's history, visit the TexasLakesTrail Region website.

TOP BOOKISH DESTINATION #10

From William Cowper Brann to Word Records and books, to Wordfest, Waco today is a book lover's paradise on the Brazos.

Waco

ANY DISCUSSION OF WACO LETTERS either begins or ends with **William Cowper Brann**. Not exactly a favorite son, Brann, an iconoclast who purchased a newspaper from **O. Henry** in Austin and moved it to Waco, was a plain-spoken and outspoken critic of **Baylor University.** Gunned down in the streets of Waco in 1898 after publicly casting aspersions on the morals of the coeds of the world's largest Baptist university, Brann has been one of the most commented-upon men of letters from Waco, and his papers can be found in the Texas Collection at Baylor.

On a more lyrical note, the Armstrong Browning Library, free and open to the public, is located on Baylor's time-honored and scenic Waco campus. The nineteenth-century research center dedicated to the study of the lives and works of Victorian poets **Robert and Elizabeth Barrett Browning** houses the world's largest collection of Browning material and other fine collections of rare 19th-century books, manuscripts, and works of art. The Library opened in 1951, the culmination of the dedication and determination of **Dr. A. J. Armstrong,** former chairman of the university's English Department, and his wife Mary Maxwell Armstrong. It has also become a popular stop for travelers and school groups who are attracted by the love story and poetry of the Brownings, or by the unique beauty of the building (below, contributed photo).

One of the state's largest poetry festivals has been held at Waco for more than two decades. The 22nd annual Beall Poetry Festival will be April 6–8 at Baylor. This three-day celebration of some of the finest contemporary poets, with readings, a panel discussion and the Virginia Beall Ball Lecture on Contemporary Poetry will feature **Kevin Young, Amaranth Borsuk,** and **Nicole Cooley** as poets and **Ernest Suarez** as critic. The festival is supported by the John A. and DeLouise McClelland Beall Endowed Fund, established in 1994 by Mrs. Virginia B. Ball of Muncie, Indiana, to honor her parents and to encourage the writing and appreciation of poetry.

Waco authors

Waco has spawned an eclectic group of authors, from the scary to the sublime to the satirical.

• **Madison Cooper,** who penned *Sironia, Texas,* a novel that describes life in the eponymous fictional town in the early twentieth century—widely thought to be a thinly disguised version of Cooper's hometown of

Waco. Weighing in at more than 1,700 pages, the book is one of the longest novels in the English language. Written over a period of 11 years, the subtle satire of upper-class Southerners was published in 1952. It won the Houghton Mifflin Literary Award and sold 25,000 copies in its initial printing, but quickly faded from public view.

- **Thomas Harris,** author of ***The Silence of the Lambs,*** was a Baylor student who covered the police beat for the Waco Tribune-Herald. The newspaper has a museum devoted to its history in downtown Waco and has a special—and growing—exhibit of former staff members who are now authors.

- Wild and crazy comedian **Steve Martin,** who grew up in Waco, has published a number of novels.

- Baylor counts more Texas governors among its alumni than any other university: **Lawrence Sullivan Ross** (1887–1891); **Pat Morris Neff** (1921–1925; Neff later served as President of Baylor from 1932 to 1947); **Price Daniel** (1957–1963), **Mark White** (1983–1987); **Ann Richards** (1991–1995). Many of these were also authors, crafting memoirs or books on public policy.

- Self-help author **Robert Fulghum,** author of nine books, including ***Everything I Really Need to Know I Learned in Kindergarten*** and ***What on Earth Have I Done?*** hails from Waco.

Word, words, and the Word

It's only fitting that a city that is home to the world's

largest Baptist university is also the birthplace of Christian literature and the Christian recording industry. **Word Records** was founded in Waco in 1951 by **Jarrell McCracken** (below, contributed photo). The label's name is based on a sixteen-minute spoken word recording written and narrated by McCracken — the first recording released by the label — titled *"The Game of Life."* McCracken, then a twenty-three-year-old KWTX sportscaster in Waco, had read an article by Jimmy Allen, a former athlete who became a Baptist preacher, and based his recording on the article (which also is called "The Game of Life").

The event is based on a full-length match between the forces of Good and Evil with Jesus Christ and Satan coaching the two teams. McCracken was familiar with play-by-play broadcasting, having created virtual baseball games for radio broadcast based on wire reports. McCracken originally presented his "Game of Life" presentation on Sunday nights at various churches around the central Texas area. Everywhere he performed it he got requests for copies. Eventually, he had a short run of records pressed to offer at churches where he spoke. The fictional radio station in the recording has the call letters "WORD," so that was printed on the label of the custom record. After being asked by a friend when he was going to release a follow-up, McCracken then decided to pursue the label on a more serious level.

By 1976, when McCracken sold part of his interest to the American Broadcasting Company, Word Records and Word Publishing had become a who's who of Christian recording and publishing. In 1992, Capital Cities ABC sold Word to Thomas Nelson, Inc. for $72 million, and Nelson made two major changes—developing the present swirling W logo (unveiled in 1995) for book products, and also moving its headquarters from Waco to its present headquarters in Nashville, Tennessee. Nelson split the record label and book publishing arms in 1996 when the labels were sold to Gaylord Entertainment. In an agreement with Gaylord, Thomas Nelson continued to use the Word Publishing" name for its book imprint until 2002, at which time it became "W Publishing Group."

Controversy and confrontation

Waco became the center of the nation's attention in 1993 when a standoff with a sect of the Branch

Davidian religious group led to a fifty-one-day siege, by the ATF, FBI, and Texas National Guard and resulted in the deaths of the Branch Davidians' leader, David Koresh, as well as eighty-two other Branch Davidian men, women, and children and four ATF agents. That standoff resulted in a spate of books about the siege, about cults, and the role of blind faith.

Waco today

These days, Waco makes our list of Top Bookish Destinations not only for its university and public libraries and its publishing history, but for its ample roster of bookstores, including Barnes & Noble; Hastings; Mardel's, Golden Books, and **Bankston's Used Books.** It's home to a chapter of the **Romance Writers of America, Sisters in Crime,** and the Waco Poetry Society. And it hosts Wordfest, one of the state's top storytelling festivals, held the last weekend of September at the city's Waco Convention Center, a riverfront facility within walking distance of the historic **Brazos River Bridge** and many downtown attractions.

Plan your visit

The city's Convention and Visitor Bureau can help you plan your visit to the area, with excellent lodging, dining, and recreation recommendations. Find them at www.WacoHeartOfTexas.com. To learn more about the area's history, visit the TexasBrazosTrail Region website.

Honorable Mention
Lubbock

LUBBOCK HAS BEEN DUBBED THE HUB CITY for being the center of a rotation of small towns in a 15-county retail trade zone that extends into Eastern New Mexico. In 2015 Lubbock County's population exceeded 300,000, and another engine behind its economic, educational—and literary—growth is **Texas Tech University,** whose enrollment surpassed 35,000 in 2015.

At a cursory glance Lubbock's famous sons and daughters might be thought of primarily writing lyrics instead of literature. Its legends include **Buddy Holly, Mac Davis, Natalie Maines** of the Dixie Chicks, and other stars whose contributions are set in stone at the **West Texas Walk of Fame** in the **Depot District.**

However, the creative writing program (begun under former Texas poet laureate **Walt McDonald**) and the Presidential lecture series at Texas Tech have brought a who's who of state and national writers to Lubbock.

And there's a growing group of local authors in a variety of genres, including **Angelina LaRue,** cookbook author, *The Whole Enchilada;* **S.J. Dahlstrom,** middle grade writer, Wilder Good series; former Tech English professor Ann Hawkins, now publishing historical romance novels as author **Rachael Miles;** poet **Janice Whittington,** and **Rene Saldaña Jr.,** with award-winning bilingual children's books.

Books set in Lubbock include *Rave On: The Biography of Buddy Holly, One Day in Lubbock, Don't Touch the Butterflies,* and *Timing.* (We'll also mention that Lone Star Literary Life, while cosmopolitan in its reach and creation, is published weekly from Lubbock by **Kay Ellington** and **Barbara Brannon,** also co-authors of the Paragraph Ranch series of novels) and NBCC critic **Michelle Newby** of Colorado City.

While Lubbock's lack of an independent full-service

bookstore has probably held it back in **Bookish Texas Destination** rankings, it boasts an excellent Barnes & Noble store (above), renowned for its dramatic two-story locale in the South Plains Mall as well as for its frequent author and book events. It's also home to **Hester Books** (used and rare) and two **Hastings** stores.

The **Lubbock Poetry Society** is active throughout the city with readings and open mic nights, and the **Write Right Critique Group** meets weekly and displays its members' books at the annual **Lubbock Arts Festival.**

Plan your visit

The city's Convention and Visitor Bureau can help you plan your visit to the area, with excellent lodging, dining, and recreation recommendations. Find them at www.VisitLubbock.com. To learn more about the area's history, visit the Texas Plains Trail Region website.

Honorable Mention
Rio Grande Valley

WHERE DOES THE RIO GRANDE VALLEY start and end? It's a wide-ranging question, and the wide range of literary contributions of cities like Laredo, McAllen, Edinburg, Harlingen, Brownsville, and Weslaco should not be overlooked.

McAllen is the smallest city in Texas (that we know of) that has its own Poet Laureate. Poets Laureate in McAllen serve one-year terms, and are selected by a group including representatives from the arts council, chamber, and city.

The Rio Grande Valley International Poetry Festival, established in 2008, is a four-day poetry festival in deep South Texas held concurrently in two countries on the last full weekend in April. V.I.P.F. is a program of Art That Heals, Inc., and El Zarape Press, with sponsorships by Creative Alignment Consulting and the McAllen Chamber of Commerce and welcomes poets from around the world.

The second Sin Fronteras Book Festival held its annual celebration of books and art for the community on March 5. In 2016 the festival was held at the McAllen Arts Incubator in McAllen. The festival showcases local presses and authors as well as visiting authors and presses from all over Texas and border cities such as Reynosa and Monterrey.

This marks the fifth year of the International Book Discussion between the Oxford School of Reynosa, Tamaulipas, Mexico, and St. Matthew's Episcopal School of Edinburg.

Thanks to the **South Texas Literacy Coalition,** educators and the participating students received a free book to read and discuss throughout the months of January and February. The STLC is a nonprofit organization dedicated to promoting and enhancing literacy throughout the South Texas region.

The **Dustin Michael Sekula Memorial Library** and the **University of Texas Rio Grande Valley** also partner to bring the Festival of International Books & Arts (FESTIBA) to Edinburg. FESTIBA is a seven-day event literacy and reading event at the University of Texas – Rio Grande Valley in Edinburg.

The Storybook Garden in Weslaco is an independent children's bookshop with storytimes, events and workshops.

A Guide to the State's Top Bookish Destinations 95

Plan your visit

Local Convention and Visitor Bureaus can help you plan your visit to the area, with excellent lodging, dining, and recreation recommendations. Find them here:

- Laredo
- McAllen
- Edinburg
- Harlingen
- Brownsville

To learn more about the area's history, visit the Texas Tropical Trail Region website.

Honorable Mention
Big Bend

2016 IS THE 100TH ANNIVERSARY of the National Park system. From Yosemite to Acadia to Big Bend, the national parks plan a yearlong celebration of events and activities. If you're going to Big Bend, it's also a great time to check out Front Street Books in Alpine and Marfa Book Company in Marfa—both represent a unique take on the local indie bookstore.

Writers find the region an inspiring place to get away from hectic city life and simply create. Perhaps that's the prime reason the Writers' League of Texas holds its annual summer retreat on the scenic campus of Sul Ross University in Alpine (right the inspiring view from the hilltop campus).

Plan your visit
The region's Convention and Visitor Bureaus can help you plan your visit to the area, with excellent lodging, dining, and recreation recommendations. Start

at www.VisitBigBend.com. To learn more about the area's history, visit the TexasMountainTrail Region website.

Readers' Favorite Bookstores 2016

TEXAS READERS HAVE SPOKEN. More than 1,000 of Lone Star Literary Life's readers cast ballots in our recent statewide contest to recognize Texas's favorite bookstores. Their selections are as diverse as the state itself, and honorees include big indies, small indies, chain stores, used bookstores, and new bookstores in every far-flung corner of the state. First-round voting began with a ballot listing all the state's 300-odd stores, and narrowed to a finalist roster of 30, The top ten vote-getters were invited to submit writeups and submit photos of their bookstores.

From the shadows of Houston's skyscrapers to the winds whistling down the plains, from the Piney Woods of East Texas to the beachside burbs on the coast, Texas bookshops are connecting with their communities, and we are thrilled to have the opportunity to showcase Texas's Top Ten Favorite Bookstores.

#1 40 Acre Wood, Lexington
521 3rd Street/ Lexington, Texas 78947

Owner: Heidi Frazier

Opened 2010

Every day that the store is open is an event! 40 Acre Wood always has hot coffee and sweets available in addition to conversation, a game of chess or two, and free advice. We're great at matching customers with books, especially remembering what a customer is looking for and subsequently finding books of interest and holding them for the customer until he can return, sometimes years later.

Recurring events at store include a Summer Reading Club — a program held every summer encouraging children to read by offering prizes, a party at summer's end, and of course, free books. We also have Halloween

Trick-or-Treating – joining other merchants in downtown Lexington on the town's square giving out candy, and of course, free books. Holds a Harry Potter trivia contest every other Halloween.

"Pass the Book" : 40 Acre Wood receives donations of books. Those who give books are asked to name a non-profit or charity that they would like to benefit. Then a small percentage of the sales of those items that sell is donated to the named charity.

Story Time is held every week to encourage each child to acquire a love of reading, a curious mind, and a personal library.

Every child receives a free book just for walking through the door (every time.)

Anyone in our community who would like a book but cannot afford one receives a book. A small book club meets sporadically to read and discuss books of self-published authors of Lexington and the surrounding communities. And I listen to my customers; they make the recommendations – usually to each other.

40 Acre Wood, a small, bookstore open 3 days per week, in a town of about 1,200 people, is home to hundreds of eclectic titles on a smattering of all subjects. It's not the books, however, that make 40 Acre Wood a great store. It's her customers, and especially the regulars.

#2 Barnes & Noble at Stonebriar Centre, Frisco

2601 Preston Rd., Suite 1204, Frisco, TX 75034

Store Manager: Jamie Lockhart; Community Business Development Manager: Nicole Caliro

Opened August 2000

Barnes & Noble Stonebriar has a group of diverse booksellers working in our store who are passionate about connecting readers with new books and new authors they will adore. If you ask each of our booksellers their favorite book, no one book will be alike (though we pretty much all love Harry Potter).

Literary and community outreach efforts in store: In addition to hosting over 100 in-store events in 2015, BN Stonebriar serves Frisco, Prosper, Little Elm, and Celina

ISDs, as well as several private schools and non-profits. We work hard to make sure we are always at the disposal of our local school districts and that all educators have a place to come and feel the love during our seasonal Educator Appreciation Events. In the 2015-2016 school year alone, Barnes & Noble Frisco has provided over 40 free author visits to local schools at several districts' elementary and middle schools.

Local Weekly Storytimes are held Thursdays at 11am; National Storytimes are held Saturdays at 11am.

We have a daily bookseller recommend on Facebook, as well as Instagram guessing games exploring the hypothetical reading lists of famous literary characters and pop culture icons. We are proud to serve one of the fastest-growing communities in the country. It is a privilege to share our love of reading with customers of all ages and bring storytimes, national events, and quality authors to the community. As booksellers, our greatest joy is putting the right book in the hands of the right reader, whether it be school reading, a gift for a loved one, or a newly discovered gem recommended by one of our booksellers- the art of bookselling and passion for reading is alive and well in this North Texas hamlet.

#3 Paragraphs on Padre Boulevard, South Padre Island

5505 Padre Boulevard, South Padre Island, TX (3 miles north of the Queen Isabella Causeway)

Owners: Joni Montover and Griff Mangan

Opened February 9, 2009

As avid readers and members of the American Booksellers Assn. Paragraphs on Padre is fairly familiar with most genres of books but most of all we love to talk about books and welcome our customer's suggestions and recommendations. We also pride ourselves on being active in the community and able to make recommendations for places to go, things to do and see, or where to eat and drink – we believe part of our role is to make sure visitors to South Padre Island have a wonderful and memorable vacation experience and so we welcome questions about the area — including the approximate time table for the free island shuttle.

We host numerous books signings and are happy to allow many self-published authors the opportunity to interact with potential readers in person. Based on participation and interest we have a Children's Storytime, monthly book club, writer's group, play reading group, and have hosted a variety of craft classes and art demonstrations. We are also a venue for the Valley International Poetry Festival every April.

We welcome groups to use our store for small gatherings or as a place to meet and discuss issues important to the community. We support many of the area's non-profit organizations with our membership and sponsorships of their fund-raising events including the El Paseo Arts Foundation, Sea Turtle Inc., Surfrider's Foundation, and the South Padre Island Birding and Nature Center. For several years we have sponsored a visiting author program with our local university. We continue to reach out and are anxious to find ways to work more efficiently with our local school districts. We donate books to the Boys and Girls Club.

Right: Griff Mangan and Joni Montover, owners (along with resident Shih Tzus)

Does staff assist in recommendations either in-store, on website, or social media? That is what we do best – recommend books. Since we like to read almost anything, including the back of cereal boxes – we will discover your interests and then help select the perfect book for your next beach read or for that special gift. We also are willing and patient enough to try to find something even the most reluctant reader will enjoy. We have an active presence on Facebook. We provide information to several local papers and currently do a book review/recommendation column for the *Coastal Current*.

As longtime visitors to South Padre Island we finally made a decision to move here and fulfill a lifetime dream of Joni's to open a bookshop. With our home located across the courtyard from the store we honestly feel like every time a customer walks into the store we are welcoming them into our home. So if you plan to come south for your beach vacation don't weigh yourself down carrying books. If you have a particular title you would like to read, give us a call and we will make sure it is here waiting for you upon your arrival. Or please, just stop in and say hello.

#4 Texas Star Trading Company, Abilene

174 Cypress St., downtown Abilene, TX

Owners: Carol and Glenn Dromgoole

Opened July 22, 2004

Texas Star Trading Company focuses on Texas books and authors, as well as Texas gifts and gourmet. We also feature autographed books and offer a good selection of Texas bargain books. Glenn Dromgoole writes a weekly newspaper and online column on Texas books and is co-founder and chairman of the West Texas Book Festival and the Texas Author Series.

Literary and community outreach efforts include gift certificates to members of Friends of the Library; Military discounts. We are one of the sponsors of the Children's Art and Literacy Festival, and promote the West Texas Book Festival and Texas Author Series.

Financial support for more than 30 community organizations.

The store hosts periodic book signings, especially featuring local authors, and participates in Independent Bookstore Day and Big Day Downtown, both in April.

Staff assist customers in recommendations either in-store, on website, or social media. We produce e-mail newsletters and Facebook postings promoting and recommending Texas books, and we answer questions and offer recommendations in-store. We also have a monthly appearance on local television promoting Texas books and authors, as well as the weekly newspaper column.

With 11 Texas flags flying outside, Texas Star Trading Company promotes itself as "The National Store of Texas," featuring Texas books, gifts, gourmet, T-shirts, and souvenirs.

#5 Barnes & Noble Dallas: Lincoln Park

7700 West Northwest Highway, Dallas, TX 75225

Manager: Craig Schlabs

Community relations manager: Cody McMahan

Opened September 1998

Barnes and Noble/Lincoln Park's management team has 152 years of bookselling experience, and all of us together have a combined total of 283 years of bookselling experience!

Storytimes are held Tuesday @ 11AM and Saturday @ 11AM. Other community events include Annual Holiday Book Drive benefiting the Reading Is Fundamental; Bookfair fundraisers benefiting schools, libraries, and arts organizations; Barnes & Noble Summer Reading Triathlon – rewarding kids for reading over the summer with free books!

We are available for recommendations in-store by phone or by Facebook message. Come join us to be a part of the best of book culture: deep levels of book and music expertise, excellence customer service and fantastic events from storytimes to author events with note worthies from the literary, political and celebrity worlds. We combine the best of your store around the corner and all the advantages of being a part of Barnes & Noble!

#6 BookPeople, Austin
603 N. Lamar Blvd., Austin TX 78703

Owned locally by BookPeople, Inc.; Steven Bercu is president of company and operates the store

Marketing director: Abby Feenewald

Opened in November, 1970

BookPeople is a general bookstore carrying a large variety of subjects, including a comprehensive kids' department, a mystery store within the store, a floor of non-fiction and another of fiction. BookPeople hosts over 500 events a year, with authors signing almost every day; story times every Tuesday, Wednesday, and Saturday. BookPeople also hosts many events offsite every month.

BookPeople is involved intensely in the community. We provide dozens of school book fairs each year and work with the regional school districts on curriculum development and author school visits. BookPeople provides the literary input for the Texas Conference for Women, the Texas Teen Book Festival, the Austin Food & Wine Festival among many others. Our literary book camps every summer attract over 1000 children from around the world. Staff recommendations are displayed all throughout the store and on our website. Staff participate in our three blogs too.

BookPeople has an two adult-book buyers, a kids'-book buyer, a remainder buyer, and a gift buyer.

BookPeople would like Lone Star Literary Life readers to know that there is no bookstore in Texas that offers an experience comparable to that they will enjoy at BookPeople. Whatever their taste, they will find an employee to talk to about that interest and be able to get recommendations about books of interest to them. It is an experience that can only be had at an independent bookstore.

#7 Recycled Books, Records, CDs, Denton
200 N. Locust, Denton, Texas

Owner: Don Foster

Community relations managers: Lacey Richins and Miles Foster

Date store opened: 1983

Recycled Books hosts recurring events at its store: Kids Summer Reading Program, Customer Appreciation Sales, 10% off purchase if customer is sporting our merchandise while shopping (shirts, tote bags, hat, etc).

Unique expertise in store: Each member of our staff has multiple areas of expertise – each of us run specific sections in the store, as well as our personal interests bleed over into helping our customers. We have staff that know all kinds of genres – books, music, and movies! We have staff that have worked here since the beginning and are able to educate on rare/collectible books. We also have an online store for the really rare/special – things on Discogs, Ebay, and Amazon. As a whole, we are a very quirky and educated bunch, and we encourage our customers to strike up conversations about books/music/movies or ask questions.

Literary and community outreach efforts in store: We continue to work with local elementary schools and supply their "Book Mobile" with children's books during the summers (they provide books to children that cannot afford to buy them). We work with the local film and music festivals, as well as the town's holiday wassail fest. We sell locally roasted coffee in our store year round, have a local area – which has both local music and local authors, do a kids summer reading program every year (in which they earn store credit to spend on more books just for reading!), and a few years ago we had a "Recycledpalooza" in which we had a benefit concert (featuring bands that the employees were a part of) to raise money for the Apple Tree Project, which provided backpacks, school supplies, clothing and shoes to children of low income families in the area.

Does staff assist in recommendations either in-store, on website, or social media? All of the above! Our staff is very diverse in their tastes, so we feel like we're able to help any customer that comes through the door. We are quick to reply to any comments/mail we receive online – we are on Facebook, Twitter, and Instagram – and we love interacting with our customers on there!

Does store have TV/radio appearance presence: We have had radio advertising in the past, and occur in a handful of TV commercials – mostly "what makes Denton, Denton"/"what makes Denton so great" representations that companies/the city puts together.

Located in an impossible-to-miss purple Opera House

on Denton's burgeoning square, Recycled Books has been a fixture of the city for over 30 years. Today the store fills every corner of the space with thousands of carefully curated books, records, CDs, movies, and collectibles. With over 500,000 books, 20,000 LPs, and 30,000 CDs and DVDs it would be difficult not to find a gift for a loved one - or a treat for yourself. It continues to attract book and music lovers to Denton—from students and locals just discovering it for the first time, to former Dentonites who adjust their nearby trips just to pass back through and visit, to dedicated collectors from all over the world who know the store always has something rare and surprising waiting for them. Come visit us on The Square, and see why Denton was voted America's best small town!

#8 River Oaks Bookstore, Houston

3270 Westheimer Rd., Houston TX

Owners: Michael and Josie Jones; Michael's mother Jeanne Jard; Community relations manager: Whitney Corson

Date store opened- 1976

River Oaks Bookstore hosts recurring events at its store: We have book signings and book clubs on a regular basis

Unique expertise in store- Jeanne is known for giving great recommendations, she has been running the bookstore for nearly 50 years – people come to chat with her, buy her recommendations, etc. She is the heart of River Oaks Bookstore!

Literary and community outreach efforts in store- yes! We do lots of in store and out of store events in the community, and offer a large selection of T

The staff is happy to recommend books, each staff member can recommend different genres of books. We also post a list of Jeanne's recommendations on the store website. The bookstore also posts news of events and happenings on Twitter and Facebook, and we email our monthly newsletter (for in store signings) to our contacts each month.

River Oaks is an independent, family owned, old fashioned bookstore. We have well-stocked shelves and well-read staff. Our store is a nice place to visit — the cookies and coffee are always here for the taking!

#9 Gladewater Books, Gladewater

109 E. Pacific, Gladewater TX 75647

Owners: Peter Adams and Elizabeth DeRieux

Date store opened: March 2007

Owners of Gladewater Books are longtime residents of Gladewater and active in the community, including in the local library, museum, and chamber of commerce. Staff assist in recommendations either in-store, on website, or social media.

We sell used books both in the store and on-line through Alibris. We have over 100,000 volumes in the store spanning a wide variety of genres, interests and price ranges. We are located in a 100+ year old building in the downtown Antique District in Gladewater. We love books and book people. The best way to reach us is to come in and see us during store hours, Tuesday – Saturday, 10:00 - 5:30. For more information people can email (ederieux@gladewaterbooks.com); call or message us on Facebook (Gladewater Books).

#10 Barnes & Noble Booksellers, Lubbock

South Plains Mall, 6002 Slide Road Lubbock, TX 79414 – 806-793-1061

Wade Whatley, Manager; Community relations manager: Terry Handley

Date store opened: Nov. 4, 2009

Barnes and Noble/Lubbock hosts recurring events at its store: Storytime (Wednesday & Saturday at 11:00 am), Mini Maker Faire (first weekend in November), Get Pop Culture (Month of July) , Dr. Seuss event (last Saturday in February), Polar Express (The first Friday evening in December)

Unique expertise in store: Education material including toys and games, digital support for our NOOK readers, literary and community outreach efforts; school

bookfairs showcasing student performances and art work, collaboration with Region 17 Education Service Center, collaboration with Literacy Lubbock and other non-profit organizations. Café serving Starbucks drinks and Cheesecake Factory cheesecake and other assorted goodies.

Does staff assist in recommendations either in-store, on website, or social media – yes in store - the current recommendation by Tyler Caughron is "The Wheel of Time Series" by Robert Jordan and on social media - Facebook, Twitter, and Instagram – BNLubbock

Terry Handley appears once a month on KLBK and discusses the events in the store, also appears on 'Trends and Friends' when large events are going on and some radio.

Barnes & Noble is the endless bookshelf. Whether you are a customer looking for a single book or a school looking for classroom sets, we have the ability to meet your needs. We provide a space for book lovers to come together to find new authors, to introduce children and teens to the joy of reading, and to reunite readers with their favorite stories and authors.

* * * * *

Major Texas book events by month

USE THIS CALENDAR OF RECURRING EVENTS and cultural emphases in Texas and those other states to plan ahead in your bookish life. We'll add dates for each year as we learn of them.

January
- National Book Month
- National Book Week (third full week of January)
- Book Publishers Day (Jan. 16 annually)
- Pulpwood Queen's Girlfriend Weekend (Nacogdoches, Jan. 14-17, 2016)

February
- Black History Month
- Lone Star Literary Life Birthday (Feb. 2 annually)
- ConDFW XV (Dallas, Feb. 12–14, 2016)

- Texas Cowboy Poetry Gathering, Alpine (February)

March
- Women's History Month
- Freedom of Information Day (March 16, 2016)
- Children's Picture Book Day (March 28 annually)
- Lone Star Literary Life's Top Ten Texas Bookish Destinations (March 6 and March 13, 2016)

April
- National Poetry Month
- D.E.A.R., "Drop Everything and Read" Month
- National Library Week (April 10-16, 2016)
- International Children's Book Day (April 2 annually)
- Children's Book Day, El día de los niños/El día de los libros (Día) (April 30, 2016)
- World Book Day (Shakespeare's birthday, April 23 annually)
- Austin International Poetry Festival (April 7-10, 2016)
- Poetry at Round Top (April 15–17, 2016)
- NETWO Spring Conference
- Houston Writers' Guild Conference
- San Antonio Book Festival (Sat, April 2, 2016)
- Texas Institute of Letters Annual Meeting (April 15–16, 2016)
- Books in the Basin (Odessa, April 9-10, 2016)

May

- Texas Writers Month
- Children's Book Week (May 4–10, 2016)
- National Independent Bookstore Day (Sat., April 30, 2016)
- O. Henry Pun-off (Austin, Sat., May 7, 2016)
- BookExpo America (Chicago, May 11-13, 2016)

June

- GLBT Books Month (starting annually in 2015)
- Bloomsday (James Joyce's Ulysses, June 16 annually)
- CALF (Children's Art & Literacy Festival), Abilene (June 9–11, 2016)
- Western Writers of America Convention (Cheyenne, Wyoming, June 21-25, 2016)
- Writers' League of Texas Agents & Editors Conference (Austin, June 24-26, 2016)
- Annual Austin African-American Book Festival (June 25, 2016)
- International Christian Retail Show (Cincinnati, Ohio, June 26-29, 2016)
- Lone Star Literary Life's Top Texas Summer and Beach Reads (June 5 and June 12, 2016)

July

- Writers' League of Texas Summer Writing Retreat (Alpine, July 17-21, 2016)

August

- East Texas Book Fest (Tyler, Aug. 26–27, 2016)
- Flor de Nopal Literary Festival (Austin)

September
- Hispanic Heritage Month (Sept. 15–Oct. 15 annually)
- Banned Books Week (last week of September annually; Sept. 25–Oct. 1, 2016)
- National Cowboy Symposium and Celebration (Lubbock, second weekend in September annually)
- West Texas Book Festival (Abilene, Sept. 19-24, 2016)
- NF 4 NF: Nonfiction for New Folks Writing Conference for Nonfiction Children's Writers (Rosenberg, Sept. 22-25)

October
- LGBT History Month
- National Friends of Libraries Week (late October annually)
- Teen Read Week (third week of October annually)
- Books in the Basin (Odessa, Oct. 11–12, 2016)
- North Texas Book & Paper Show (Grapevine)

November
- Native American Heritage Month
- National Novel Writing Month
- University Press Week (November 2016)
- Texas Book Festival (Austin, Nov. 5–6, 2016)

December
- World AIDS Day (Dec. 1 annually)

A WORD TO THE LITERARY TRAVELER

Thanks for taking our tour of Literary Texas 2016. We know there are many more great literary destinations in the state, some of which we covered in our 2015 online edition and many more of which we've visited and are eager to write about.

If you have suggestions, or know of any closings or openings, please email us: info@LoneStarLiterary.com

Lone Star Literary Life is the weekly online newspaper for all things bookish in Texas, from reviews and interviews to industry news to the most comprehensive weekly calendar of literary events statewide. We invite you to subscribe (for free), read (we publish weekly, on Sunday afternoons), and share. Our mix of editorial and advertising content is designed to inform, educate, and inspire — and to recognize the great literary traditions and contributions of our state.

ABOUT THE EDITORS

A veteran of the news industry and a Texas native, **Kay Ellington** knows Texas books and readers—and marketing. She is an alum of the Kenyon Writers' Workshop and the co-author, with Barbara Brannon, of the Paragraph Ranch series of novels.

Barbara Brannon's career in books and publishing, and teaching spans three decades. She works full-time in heritage tourism, traveling miles and miles of Texas.

A member of the National Book Critics Circle, **Michelle Newby** is a reviewer for *Kirkus Reviews*, freelance writer, blogger at www.TexasBookLover.com, and a moderator at the 20th annual Texas Book Festival. Her reviews appear in *Pleiades Magazine, Rain Taxi, World Literature Today, High Country News, South85 Journal, The Review Review, Concho River Review, Monkeybicycle, Mosaic Literary Magazine, Atticus Review,* and *The Collagist*.

www.ingramcontent.com/pod-product-compliance
Lightning Source LLC
Chambersburg PA
CBHW071739080526
44588CB00013B/2093